THE CYCLE TOURERS' HANDBOOK

Tim Hughes

THE CYCLE TOURERS' HANDBOOK

B.T. Batsford Ltd · London

ISBN 0 7134 5136 X

Typeset by Keyspools Ltd, Golborne, Lancs
and printed in Great Britain by
Anchor Brendon Ltd
Tiptree, Essex
for the publishers
B. T. Batsford Ltd
4 Fitzhardinge Street
London W1H 0AH

CONTENTS

A healthy pastime, the freedom to enjoy the sights and sounds of the countryside and an economical form of personal transport are just three of the benefits which are helping to make cycling ever more popular. It is something which can be enjoyed by all ages as individuals, families or groups. Tim Hughes is a well-known cycling journalist and an experienced member of the Cyclists' Touring Club. The sound advice offered by him in this handbook is welcomed and I am sure will be helpful, particularly to those new to the pastime, in opening wide the doors of a very simple, enjoyable and friendly world.

Ivy Thorp
President of the Cyclists' Touring Club

FOREWORD

It is not the purpose of this book to sell high-priced cycle equipment. In any case, the 'ultimate' component often just isn't appropriate for cycle-touring anyway. For example, you could pay well into three figures for a chainwheel set with all the titanium fancy bits, but you wouldn't be able to fit the small chainwheels that the cycle-tourist needs. One a quarter the price would actually do the job better. This book costs a lot less even than that—in fact, about the same as a 5- or 6-speed freewheel; if it saves you buying a freewheel with altogether the wrong ratio, it will have served at least part of its purpose.

The author has no connection with any cycle equipment manufacturer, importer or retailer; where specific makes or items are recommended it is entirely on the basis of personal or collective experience. Such advice has been deliberately kept on the conservative side, avoiding unproved ideas and novelties. Reliability has been a major consideration. The intention throughout has been to ensure that nobody can in any way go wrong by following the information given. Nevertheless, my way is often only one of several right ones. You may well, after a bit of experience want to be a bit more adventurous or experimental with your equipment; do not, however, forget the purpose of it all, which is to travel by bicycle comfortably, safely and—most of all—enjoyably. It is all too easy to be diverted into being an equipment-and-theoretical-perfection freak, to the exclusion of actually doing any cycling.

INTRODUCTION

In one form or another bicycles have been present for nearly 150 years. Before 1880 organised cycling clubs and national organisations had been formed, among their objects the promotion of touring by bicycle. By 1900 lady bicyclists had written of their round-the-world travels, made possible by the invention of the 'safety' bicycle.

For a short time the bicycle had been the fastest vehicle on the road. High society had taken to it: in 1891 the Cambridge University Bicycle Club was the largest club in the country. With the coming of the motor car the bicycle moved down-market. H. G. Well's *Wheels of Chance*—one of cycling's relatively rare appearances in fiction—describes how the humble draper's assistant Mr Hoopdriver took to the road and made the acquaintance of the The Girl in Grey, far above his station.

There is no doubt that up to, and in some places just after, the Second World War, the bicycle was one of the great emancipators of the working class. Large numbers of cyclists took to the road from industrial towns which the bicycle had suddenly brought nearer to the open spaces and clean air of the Dales or Peak District, to the South Downs or rural Warwickshire. For many the bicycle brought with it opportunities to appreciate natural beauty and reinforced desires for self-education and advancement.

There was something of a cycling boom just after the Second World War as austerity relaxed and affluence had not yet made the motor car the universal possession it is today. Cycling numbers inevitably declined after this as those for whom the bicycle had been no more than a means of transport took to the increasingly attainable car.

But within twenty years there came the first signs of a reversal of the trend, beginning in—of all places—the USA. Worries about pollution, of the finite nature of fossil fuel supplies and of the perils of physical indolence all contributed. The new wave of cyclists was essentially middle-class, educated and articulate; and, as with so many things American, the trend spread to Britain and Europe. Cycle campaign groups,

working towards the achievement of local and wider cycle schemes, have become widespread. Urban cyclists abound. The Cyclists' Touring Club—founded as the Bicycle Touring Club in Harrogate in 1878, the first touring club of any kind in the world—has seen its membership climb again from the 1970 trough of about 18,000. At the time of writing, this number has more than doubled.

By 'cycle-touring' we mean all forms of non-competitive cycling for leisure and travel, from half an hour through the park to a round-the-world trip. It embraces many different types of bicycle—you can enjoy cycling, up to a point, on almost any—but for self-sufficient, reliable, all-weather transport one or two have advantages. This book will steer you, so to speak, in the right direction.

But what *is* the special appeal of the bicycle? Why do so many cyclists seem to be only just on the healthy side of fanaticism? Why indeed do they ride bicycles?

It is all too easy to give the *Boy's-Own-Paper* kind of answer—the virtues of the brisk cold shower and the healthy self-denying open-air life; and of course there *is* an element of that. It *is* a congenial form of healthy exercise. There *is* an achievement in reaching the distant destination, the craggy pass, unaided. And indeed—though I doubt if the average cyclist would admit it directly—there *is* something not far from spiritual uplift as you take a new road towards the hills, as you glimpse the first snow-capped peak, as the road starts to climb and the valley closes in. And there is even pleasure, a little ironic perhaps, but well short of masochism, in taking on the elements on their own ground, in overcoming your own weaknesses.

There is also something the cycle-tourist shares with the rambler: it's as though the walker had been given the blessing of the seven-league boots of mythology, but was still able to travel at a human pace, seeing, hearing, sensing and smelling, but not—largely—disturbing the essential countryside.

For many newer cyclists there is desirability in the concept, the nature, of the bicycle itself. Its manufacture makes no great demands on energy or material

resources; its use calls for no irreplaceable fuel; it is the ultimate non-polluting vehicle.

For yet others the bicycle is, or began as, an affordable form of transport as an adjunct to other activites, to visit places or things in which they have a special interest. What better than the almost silent bicycle to potter round old churches or the remnants of long-gone civilisations?

For some, cycling—and not necessarily organised cycling—is a path to companionship. It often seems that cycle-touring as a pastime has more than its share of lone and sometimes lonely people. For them there is reality in the clichéd fellowship of the open road.

All of these have part of the answer—none alone has it all. But whatever your first interest in cycling, don't count up the miles, nor even the hours, just enjoy it.

Fig. 1 The lure of the open road—a well-worn cliché that's nevertheless true

11

ONE

CYCLING COMFORT AND SAFETY

Probably the two main factors which deter people from even considering cycling as a pastime are fears of discomfort and danger—the latter principally from other traffic. We ought to dispel the fears immediately. Comfort, particularly, depends on coddling the human motor, so we begin by looking at that.

The human motor

By the standard of even the smallest of motor cycles, the human body is terribly underpowered. The flat-out effort, possibly kept up for only a matter of seconds, is of the order of 1HP, say 750w. A comfortable effort you can maintain for hours is a mere fraction, perhaps a fifth to a tenth of this. That this delicate motor can carry cyclists to the ends of the earth is a tribute to the bicycle mechanism's efficiency.

The secret is that the bicycle supports part of the rider's weight. The longer the effort, the greater the effect. For example, over a distance of 200m the best cyclists, even when allowed a flying start, are only about twice as fast as the best runners. At 24 hours, the British bicycle record—which many people don't realise to be as high as 507.00 miles (or 815.92km)—is rather over three times as far as the best runner can manage. And when it comes to the 1350km or so from Land's End to John o'Groats, the cyclist's 1 day 21 hours 3 minutes is nearly six times faster than the running record.

Muscular tissues have a subtle mix of components some of which work best under slow and others under faster contraction conditions. At extreme effort the racing cyclist makes full use of the faster elements, pedalling to perhaps 120rpm, certainly over 100 for long spells. The touring cyclist isn't in the same league but, even so, a fairly brisk pedalling rate is the most effective and the most comfortable. Although the flexible human motor can misleadingly offer near its maximum torque at very low pedalling rates, as when starting off, it seems to be happiest at moderate road speeds of about 20kph (12mph) when turning the

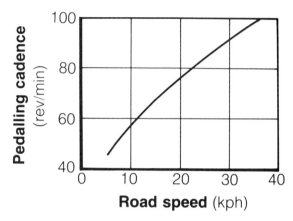

Fig. 2 Pedalling rate or cadence at different road speeds, based on observation of experienced touring cyclists

pedals at around 70rpm. At, say, 7kph (4.5mph)—the sort of speed you might use up a fairly steep hill—somewhere near 50rpm feels right. At higher speeds it feels more natural to pedal faster, say 90rpm at speeds around 30kph (18.6mph). These pedalling rates are not in proportion to the road speeds, which means that it is necessary to vary the distance travelled per pedal resolution. This is where variable gearing comes in. Simple calculation shows that 7kph at 55rpm requires you to cover about 2m for each turn of the pedals, while 90rpm at 30kph calls for nearly 6m a turn—which suggests a ratio of some 3 to 1 between largest and smallest gears for ease and comfort. Because this subject is so important it has a large section to itself in Chapter 3 (pp 36–41) where we learn how to achieve such a gear range in practice.

The likelihood of meeting hills is one of the imagined deterrents to cycling, but sensible gearing—together with the cultivation of a certain patience—allows them to be conquered, almost with ease. Certainly some degree of unevenness in the landscape is generally more attractive than the utterly flat. Chapter 14 goes into more detail on climbing techniques.

Leaving aside the slowing effect of going uphill,

Fig. 3 Two routes to a streamlined machine: the 'Flying Greenhouse' fairing round a conventional racing tandem (almost uncontrollable in a side wind) and a Dutch 'human-powered vehicle'—an enclosed tricycle in which the rider pedals from a supine position

what is it, then, that limits the cyclist's speed? The answer lies principally in wind resistance. Rolling resistance, which combines all the frictional elements of the rotating bearings on the bicycle, plus power losses in the transmission and by the subtle and continuous deformation of the tyres, is relatively small. Scientific estimates put the power requirement to overcome this on a typical touring bicycle at about 15w at 16kph, 30w at 32kph and so on—it increases linearly with speed. Obviously there are differences between types of bicycle, and between well-maintained and neglected ones. The power requirements for overcoming wind resistance do not progress in this gentlemanly fashion, but increase with the cube of the air speed. The basic resistance to wind also varies, very markedly, with riding position and intrinsic size: these represent changes in the drag coefficient of the rider and machine. The cube-law increase means, though, that whereas at 16kph the power requirements to overcome wind resistance may be of the same order as the rolling resistance, 15w, by 32kph it is 2^3, i.e. 8 times higher; by 48kph it is 27 times greater. Head winds have a similar effect. At this punitive rate of increase the 75w human motor soon runs out of steam.

Reducing the drag of the machine is a thriving area of human endeavour and special machines, some bizarre, some elegant, but few looking like bicycles, have been devised which allow riders, usually supine, to get well over the 90kph mark for timed sprints. Unfortunately the lying position and the enclosed streamlining make visibility out, visibility to others, steerability, susceptibility to side winds and ventilation too poor, for the most part, for a practicable road vehicle. But there could be some interesting spin-offs in bicycle design from these enthusiasts' machines.

People's efficiencies at turning food into movement energy also vary, and so do their natural power outputs. Each rider thus has a natural rhythm, a function of this power, which determines a natural comfortable cruising speed. On the flat, in still air, these natural speeds usually lie between 15 and 25kph (9–15mph). When planning your first trips assume that your ability lies towards the bottom end of the scale and take it gently.

Finally, the human motor needs fuel. The steady 75w, 1/10HP, kept up for 8 hours at a reasonable metabolic efficiency of 20 per cent calls for something like 2500 kilocalories. What you eat is largely a matter of taste, though little and often seems to be better than infrequent large meals while you're on the road. Riding on a very full stomach is about as uncomfortable as riding on a very empty one. It's probably best to leave the day's main meal until you stop for the night. Because the human engine's cooling system works by sweating, moisture will need to be replaced. The simplest of drinks—water, or perhaps fruit juices—are the best to carry with you, the moist foods are more appealing than dry ones.

Often a sort of hunger fatigue (a drastic lowering of the blood sugar) can creep up on you: British club cyclists term it 'bonk' or 'hunger knock'; French ones attribute it to the man with the hammer. The symptoms are muscles like jelly and cold sweats. The immediate cure is to take a rest with perhaps a *little* honey, sugar or glucose and then to eat some longer-burning food.

Perhaps the best recipe for keeping the human engine content is to follow the handed-down 'Rules of *Velocio*'. *Velocio* was the *nom-de-vélo* of Paul de Vivie who evangelised for the pastime of cycle-touring ('The apostle of the variable gear', reads his memorial near St Etienne) in France from about 1890 until his death in 1930. Among his precepts were: stop before you are tired, eat before you are hungry, drink before you are thirsty (but no red wine on the road!), change down a gear before it gets hard, and don't be afraid to expose your body to the fresh air when it gets warm. Seventy years on, the advice is as valuable as ever.

Riding position

The 'dropped' handlebars of the 'racing' bicycles have the advantage of allowing you to achieve a range of comfortable riding positions. You have five points of personal contact with the bicycle: two hands, two feet and one seat taking varying proportions of your weight. The static proportions are then modified by how hard you pedal.

A racing cyclist, flat out with hands on the drops, is likely actually to be pulling on the bars so that the legs work against a stronger reactive force. The saddle is little more than a guide. This explains why short-distance sprinters can accept a saddle which has the shape and hardness of half a milk bottle—they're not putting any weight on it. At the other extreme, somebody freewheeling in carefree fashion down a steady hill could have nearly all their weight on the saddle.

The whole art of positioning is to distribute your weight in the best way. We shall discuss the technicalities of this in Chapter 4.

The most comfortable touring position is one that brings your back about 45 degrees to the horizontal, or a shade more upright for normal riding (Fig. 4). This is best achieved by assuming that you will adopt either positions 2 or 3 for most riding on the flat or gently up

Fig. 4 The four possible riding positions

or down hill. The two are interchangeable and offer you alternative hand positions to give a little variety which helps to prevent discomfort in the hands, arms and shoulders through holding them too long in one posture. Note that in position 2 the hands will normally be resting on the brake levers, which are best fitted with natty rubber hoods for the purpose.

This leaves position 1, the racer's crouch, for use when you really do need to reduce your frontal area into a headwind or to hurry on the flat (going uphill the sitting-up positions are better). Unless you are pushing quite hard on the pedals, though, too much of your weight will be on your hands, leading possibly to numbness and neck ache.

Position 4 at one time, though far less today, divided cyclists into two armed camps. Derogatory epithets were hurled from the battlements, while the scenes when the first rider in Britain won a hill-climb race *without sitting in the saddle* were altogether remarkable. It's not a terribly elegant way of riding, although the romantic French call it *en danseuse*, far-fetchedly likening it to a ballerina on her points. The less poetic British term it 'honking'.

The technique involves rising out of the saddle, while holding the brake lever hoods, and applying the whole body weight to each pedal in turn by standing on it. It needs a certain amount of experience and practice to do it and keep going straight. It can only be done at relatively low pedalling speeds, something like 60 and below. The main uses of 'honking' are when you are faced with a sudden, maybe unexpected, short climb, when accelerating from a low speed, or when you're caught in too high a gear—baulked by other traffic, say, or faced with a sudden canal bridge. Although effective in getting power to the pedals it's fairly profligate of

energy and difficult to sustain. It also puts quite heavy sideways stresses on the front wheel. It's a perfectly legitimate expedient and can be very useful, but if you find you are spending long spells out of the saddle, you're using too high gears or your basic position is incorrect.

Fig. 5 There is virtually no springing on a bicycle, so you need to keep elbows slightly bent and wrists flexible, as this rider is doing in a long-distance trial—where day-long comfort is essential. On rough stretches ankles and knees are used in the same way to keep weight off the saddle

There is basically no springing on a bicycle. There is a certain amount of shock absorption at tyres (most), in front forks and wheels and saddle top. The real 'suspension' comprises the flexible joints at the rider's knees and ankles, elbows and wrists. So, one of the comfort techniques is keeping elbows slightly bent and flexible, with a light pull on the bars, and knees and ankles poised to suspend you just clear of or only lightly on the saddle, on any bumpy surface. Once you can do it you will have a sensation of the bicycle floating up and down below you, following the road surface, while your body continues smoothly along unbounced and unbouncing. If you ride with your elbows straight, particularly on the drops, with a lot of weight on your hands, you will soon feel the characteristic ache across the base of the back of the neck, between the shoulder blades. Having to hold your head up from a low position makes it worse. You might think that a solution would be to use fat plastic handlegrips on the handlebars but, generally, if you feel the need for such padding you should first take a very close look at your position and your riding technique.

The final skill is the acquisition of a good riding style—one in which the upper body is almost motionless while the legs rotate smoothly and evenly. Stylish riders progress without apparent effort—very demoralising for the opposition. The enemies of good style are gears which are too high, a saddle too high or too low and feet in the wrong place on the pedals. The ball of the foot should be directly above the pedal bearing and toeclips and straps help. Details of how you achieve the right placings appear in Chapter 4.

Aches and pains

Apart from long-forgotten muscles registering their token protest at being brought into action, most cycling aches and pains result from poor riding position, or abuse of body or equipment.

Muscular injuries are rare among cyclists, even racing ones. Inflamed tendons are less so: tendonitis has become the fashionable reason for pulling out of the Tour de France. The root cause is overloading of the knee and ankle joints by using too-high gears—often compounded in racing by using extra-long cranks for more leverage. This bends the knee too far. For the non-competitive cyclist the only real cure is a few days off the bicycle; the preventive measure is to learn to pedal more gently and more rapidly. Too low a saddle over-flexes the knee joint and leads to a characteristic ache in the lower half of the quadriceps muscle on top of the thigh. The rolling-around on the saddle brought on by too high a saddle placing is usually too uncomfortable to pass unnoticed.

Knee and ankle joint pains can also result from a bent crank or pedal axle. You should check the bicycle after any fall. Handlebars, brakes, pedals and so on should normally be set up symmetrically (but see Chapter 10).

The characteristic and diagnostic ache between the shoulder blades through having too much weight on the hands and/or arms held too straight has already been mentioned. Other back troubles can arise from too stretched a position, often aggravated by exposing the kidney area to cold passing air.

Too much weight on the hands can also result in wrist ache. General friction-induced hand soreness, which seems to affect some people more than others, can be avoided by using 'track mitts', fingerless leather-palmed gloves.

Saddle comfort

Saddle soreness figures prominently in the outside world's cycling mythology, the source of many misconceptions. Nevertheless, saddle discomfort can be painful, highly offputting and even embarrassing. The principal symptoms are bruising (or too much pressure on too small an area) and chafing of thighs or genital areas.

A bicycle saddle supports you mainly at two points, the ischial bones, distinct bony bosses at the base of the large pelvic bone. However, a small but subtly important proportion is also borne by the softer parts of the perineum in between. The broad part of the saddle must be wide enough to support the ischial bones properly. It it is too narrow it will try to wedge the bones apart which is agonising. The distance between the two bones varies between individuals and between males and females; you can make a rough check on the bones' position by feel but the only real test is to sit on a saddle.

The part of the saddle you sit on should be fairly firm but resilient: a moderate thumb pressure should depress it appreciably but the surface should spring back as soon as you let go. If it's too hard the ischial bones will bounce up and down or you will put too much pressure on them, resulting in pressure spots or bruising. This back part of the saddle should be gently convex to give the desirable ischial bone/perineum balance of support.

Too soft a saddle, one that's sloppily sprung, or one that's intrinsically too wide in the middle and front part, can cause chafing on the inside of the thighs. Often it isn't until your weight is on it that it spreads.

Once more, personal dimensions and tolerances vary and you may have to try several different models.

The extremely personal discomfort of genital chafing arises generally from the nose or peak of the saddle rubbing or pressing. Some riders, particularly females, have reported shorter saddles to be more comfortable. It's only fair to point out, though, that many women are perfectly happy with conventional ones. A riding position which makes your body lean forward more than about 45 degrees in the 'on-the-tops' cruising position (possibly even a little more upright for women) and having the saddle set up more than a degree or so away from the horizontal makes matters much worse.

The most comfortable saddles, then, have several factors in common: adequately wide and gently convex when viewed from the rear, rapidly tapering to a relatively narrow peak when seen from above, and gently concave when looked at from the side. It's difficult to describe exactly, but there's a feeling of sitting *in*, rather than on, a truly comfortable saddle. The appropriate section in Chapter 4 (p44) looks at the types available. Once you've found the saddle of your dreams, cherish it—sell the bike and buy a better one if you will, but keep the saddle. I'd even suggest buying two such saddles (or more) as provision for the future!

Fig. 6 Anatomy of a comfortable saddle

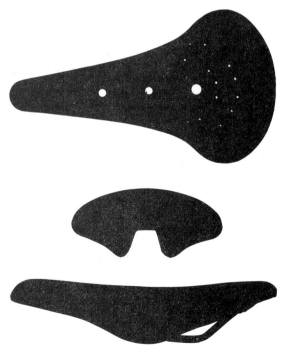

Not all seat discomfort can be blamed on the saddle, however. Riding position plays its part, but so do how tired you are and your clothing. The proportion of your weight borne by arms, legs and seat varies with how hard you push on the pedals. As your legs become wearier, so they carry a smaller share of your weight, putting more of it on the saddle. Chafing also obviously gets worse the longer it goes on, so that it is at the end of a ride that an unsuitable saddle is going to become less and less comfortable.

Clothing which does not stretch, is too tight or has seams in the wrong places is also going to make matters worse. Denim jeans followed or accompanied by unsuitable underwear are perhaps the most common culprits. Shorts or trousers specially designed for cycling and with the appropriate linings can make a tremendous difference.

The weather

One of the deeper-seated fears of the non-cyclist concerns rain. 'What do you do if it rains?' they ask. Chapter 8, on clothing, looks at the 'waterproof' garments available, but it is only fair to state at this stage that there is no way of remaining *absolutely* dry on a bicycle in the rain.

Being wet, on its own is no real discomfort; the real enemy is *cold* and the chilling effect of being wet. Cyclists are particularly susceptible to this because of the relatively high air speeds induced by cycling, even more noticeable when not making any warming effort when freewheeling down a long hill. In these conditions it is easy to reach air speeds of 50 to 55kph—equivalent to a full gale. The two graphs of this 'wind chill factor' show the effects of air speed on effective temperature, particularly the enormous influence of moisture. The difference in air speed also explains why it is much colder riding *into* a chilly headwind than *with* it.

One obvious protection against getting wet—apart from capes, cagoules and so on—is to ensure that the bicycle is fitted with efficient full-length mudguards, preferably with a 'mudflap' at the bottom of the front one to keep water off your feet (and at the same time off the chain and gears). The tell-tale stripe of road dirt up the backs of riders who ride in the rain without them should be warning enough. What you don't see is the added discomfort of sitting in what feels like a pool of wet sand.

But it is not only from outside that moisture comes. The human motor's delicate heat balance is controlled by sweating. As body temperature rises sweat is exuded onto the skin surface and the heat needed for

Fig. 7 Mountains can be at their most imposing in changeable weather—but beware of letting yourself get chilled

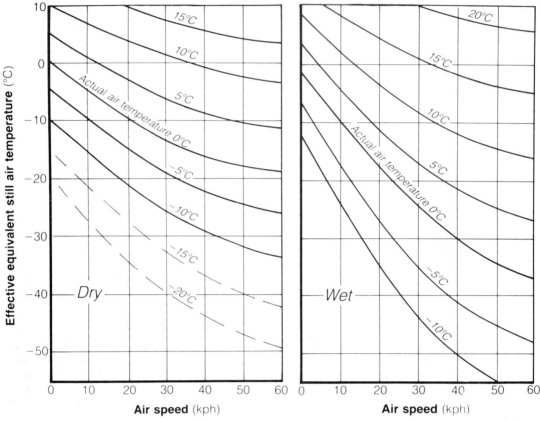

Fig. 8 The effect of wind chill, *(left)* under dry conditions, *(right)* if the body, clothing or atmosphere is wet. Each curve represents an actual air temperature, while the left-hand axis shows the equivalent still air temperature at a given air speed. The air speed can be the result of a breeze, of the rider's speed through still air or a combination of the two. Note and beware the dramatic effect of moisture. (Curves derived from tabulated figures: source—J. and V. van der R. Krausz, The Bicycling Book (Dial Press, New York, 1982))

the passing airstream to evaporate it is drawn from the body, so cooling it. The problem in cycling is to strike a balance. In hot weather there's little problem since you don't get chilled and sweat evaporates easily from exposed skin. All you need to do is drink enough to make up the water loss. It's on cool and cold days— below about 10–15°C (50–59°F)—that it becomes more difficult. Metabolisms vary so there are no precise rules. You should ensure that your clothing is porous enough to allow any sweat to evaporate but staunch enough to avoid wind chill, a condition best met by several thin layers of wool or wool-like knits. Chapter 8 goes into more detail.

Clothing made especially for cycling is cut to allow ready leg movement and, because a forward-leaning position tends to expose the lower back, cycling tops are longer at the back, and cycling shorts and trousers higher-waisted than normal clothing.

Hands, ears, forehead and feet can get much colder than when you are standing still. Do not be surprised if you find you need gloves, for example, at quite high ambient temperatures.

Hot weather calls for fewer precautions, at least in Britain. The American cycling organisation, Bikecentennial, which runs long-distance organised tours in the USA and Canada, maintains that more people leave their trips prematurely from sunburn than from any other cause. You could be forgiven for thinking in an average British summer that the mere *chance* of getting sunburnt would make a welcome change. Even so, forearms, the back of the neck and any exposed part of the shoulders and back are particularly vulnerable. They are held in much the same position, poised to catch the sun, for quite long periods. Often the early stages of burning are masked by the cooling effect of the passing air. The natural coolness of the air at high altitudes can mislead in the same way. Experienced riders in hot countries often wear thin but long-sleeved and collared shirts, at least for the first few days. Ultraviolet screening creams are also useful.

Safety

Cycling safety is like safety in most other circumstances: a matter of commonsense and largely dependent on your own behaviour—even where other traffic is involved.

Those parts of the bicycle which govern its control—brakes, steering, tyres and transmission—should be in first-class condition. Basic maintenance is covered in Chapter 11. Unless you can stop, steer, accelerate and corner with confidence, more refined techniques count for little. You must learn the capabilities of your brakes and roadholding in the wet as well as the dry. Loads should be carried so that they don't sway or foul the chain, brakes, wheels or steering. Clothing should be close-fitting enough not to catch in any part of the mechanism. Chapter 14 goes into more detail on the basic elements of riding technique.

Most safety is simply a matter of *not* doing what could turn out to be dangerous. In the absence of other traffic, speed should match the conditions. The amount of energy you have to dissipate to come to a stop varies as the square of your speed: it's four times harder to stop from 40kph than from 20. It is enormously exhilarating, and reasonably safe, to let the bicycle have its head and go fast down an open moorland road with no sheep, few bends and on a clear dry day. It would be patently stupid to do the same thing in a wet mist on a narrow winding road on the outskirts of a town.

There are always potential hazards to be anticipated—and learned by experience. How sharp is the bend at the foot of the hill? Is the barking dog in the farm confined or is it going to rush into your path? Is that rough patch you can see ahead just a little bumpy or does it conceal serious potholes? All these—and many more—call, not for sudden braking or swerving, but a readiness to slow and take the obstacle gently. Safe cycling shouldn't be a trail of trepidation, but you need to develop, to the point of instinct, an awareness of potential hazards.

When there is other traffic on the road you need even more alertness; and you must learn above all to behave predictably, not to surprise other road users by some unexpected move. A driver or another cyclist should be able to discern your next move from your position on the road and what you are doing.

It is the difference in speed between the bicycle and other traffic that causes problems. Nobody gets run down by a car that's travelling at the same speed and in the same direction as they are. In heavy traffic there are two possible styles of riding that you can adopt, depending on how fast you're going relative to the rest. Chapter 15 covers them and also urban cycling in some detail.

Cycling in heavy traffic is not very pleasant—although riders have been known to admit that they ride in weekday London partly 'because it's so exciting'! Nevertheless, noise, smell and the wind buffeting you get from fast passing vehicles, as much as the fear of collision, make main-road cycling unattractive. In addition, the wide open spaces, gradients, junctions and the ever-increasing road furniture are all designed with the fast-moving motorist in mind. The modern trunk road is a windswept and desolate place, and it is better to choose a route—everyday urban or holiday rural—which takes you away from traffic. Chapter 15 gives points to watch in planning a regular urban route, while Chapter 16 shows how maps can be used in the countryside to pick out attractive and traffic-free routes.

The final safety topic is that of protective clothing. This is an emotive subject and appears to arouse fierce disagreement; it must be up to individuals to determine their own standpoint. At one extreme lie those who make the claim that responsibility for avoiding collision is entirely that of the overtaking vehicle, which should as a matter of principle be driven in such a manner that it can be stopped before it collides with anything foreseen or unforeseen. This is undoubtedly morally true—and should be the starting point of legislation—but as a precept for practical behaviour it ignores the known failing of human nature.

The cyclist at the opposite extreme feels that all drivers are to a greater or lesser extent out to get him and that the only answer is to wear heavily padded clothes and gloves and a helmet, together with fluorescent belts and anklets, and to fit to the bicycle a reflective wand which sticks out to the offside to warn passing cars to keep their distance. This, claim the protagonists of the first part, transfers the onus on preserving life from the potential assailant to the potential victim, a morally untenable thesis. Furthermore, they say, widespread adoption of such measures is likely to lead, first, to drivers looking out only for cyclists decorated in this fashion and, subsequently, to demands that such fitments be made compulsory. There are certainly precedents.

As with all arguments which lead to extreme postures the pragmatic answer lies in the ill-defined ground between. The embodiment in the law and, more importantly, in the public social conscience, of the principle extended by the first group is obviously something that should be worked for. But we are here concerned with survival—and, well beyond that, with enjoyment—while cycling in today's imperfect world. There is no doubt that light and colourful clothing does make the cyclist more conspicuous to other road users; it *is* doubtful whether fluorescent belts worn with camouflage olive, drab, dark brown, midnight blue or black are any better. There is no doubt that a helmet can protect you from some injuries if you fall— from quite nasty abrasions, certainly; there *is* real doubt that it offers protection against potentially fatal or brain-damaging impacts. Remember that any head-gear modifies hearing and that some helmets restrict peripheral vision. Nevertheless, if you feel so insecure without, say, a helmet, that your confidence and pleasure in cycling would be destroyed, then one can hardly counsel you to discard it. What I would seriously caution against, though, is belief that any of these devices is a magic talisman conferring immunity from injury. Predictable behaviour and commonsense are far more important and effective.

TWO

TYPES OF BICYCLE

Bicycles have basically all evolved from the same historical root. The very early bicycles were driven directly: the pedal cranks were fixed to the front wheel and one turn of the pedals gave one turn of the wheel. As designs became more refined it became necessary to increase the size of the front wheel to enable the newly mobile bicyclist to travel further for each revolution. Eventually the size of the wheel was limited by the length of the rider's legs to somewhere around 150cm (60in); this was the apotheosis of the high Ordinary Bicycle, about 100 years ago.

The next stage was quite innovatory: instead of driving directly to the front wheel, the pedals were connected to the back one by means of a chain. Because this allowed some gearing-up, the actual size of the wheel no longer determined the distance of travel, and wheel sizes came down again. This brought the rider's position much nearer the ground, and so decreased the risk of falling that the new invention was billed as the Safety Bicycle. Both wheels were about the same size and the basic layout was very roughly the shape familiar today.

The lower position and the newly-invented pneumatic tyre allowed higher speeds, and racing bicycles evolved with downward curved handlebars to allow a crouched wind-cheating position. The utility bicycle has changed little from the basic 'safety' design and continues today as the roadster, the staple of Asia, Africa and countries where the bicycle is a common mode of transport. The touring bicycle borrowed much from the racing world but with slightly heavier-duty components—for reliability—and features such as mudguards and carriers and bags.

Some 40 to 30 years ago one could have said that there was little basic difference between a bicycle frame used for racing and one for touring. The differences would have been entirely in the components added, particularly the wheels and tyres. Nowadays frame designs have become more specialised. Track racing bicycles—with no freewheel and no brakes—have always been a quite distinct breed. Time-trial bicycles, after reaching near idiocy in close

Fig. 9 The apotheosis of the front-wheel-drive direct-gear bicycle—an Ordinary from the early 1880s. The single direct gear was limited by the size of wheel the rider could straddle ·

clearances and steep angles, seem now to be concentrating on 'low-profile' frames designed to reduce wind resistance.

Cycle-tourists no longer have to accept the racers'

23

Fig. 10 Roadster bicycle design doesn't change much. These two 'vintage' between-the-wars models could have been made 30 years earlier—or 50 later

cast-offs. Variable gears to suit the leisure cyclist's needs have been developed; a new variety is available in bags and carriers, and other components have subtly changed. The bicycle illustrated in Fig. 11 is somewhere near the consensus view of what is suitable for touring. The frame angles are a little shallower than those of the out-and-out racing machine, there is room to fit mudguards and comfortable tyres, gears are lower and more numerous, and the saddle and handlebar positions a little more relaxed. Of the novel designs that have emerged over the last few years only one or two have made any dent in the claim of this type to be the best for the job.

The first is the brainchild of one man, engineer Dr Alex Moulton. His was the first of the spate of small-wheel designs and the only one to be a true lightweight machine. The latest version incorporates a multi-triangulated frame of smaller-diameter tubes, 43cm (17in) wheels, sprung suspension and various load carriers which exploit the space low down permitted by the small wheels. The whole concept is an ingenious solution to a number of engineering problems, some of which, it must be said, are self-imposed.

The second type is still in its relative infancy. It is known under several names—'mountain bike' (a registered trade mark in the USA), 'all-terrain bike', 'off-road' bike—all of which partly describe it. The gears, chainwheel set and several other components come straight from current lightweight designs (some upgraded and others glamorised with an off-road image). The lay-back frame, the upright riding position and the wide wheels (65mm (2½in) and 45mm (1¾in) tyre

24

Fig. 11 A conventional modern touring bicycle—but all is not what it seems because this is a specially-built small 45cm frame model with 600 (24in) wheels and short cranks. It doesn't actually look particularly small because almost everything is reduced in proportion. Chapter 3 looks at the all-important subject of making the bicycle size fit you.

sections) are lightweight developments of motor-cycle and roadster ideas.

Its main protagonists see it rather in the same light as skis: one would take one's mountain bike to a mountain and use it entirely off the road, for fun or competitively. Others are using them for more conventional cycle-touring in strenuous and rough country—and they cross some types of rough ground with a lot more ease than a conventional bicycle.

One suspects that two divergent types may emerge: the high-tech off-the-road-only specialised machine, and some sort of hybrid between the current mountain bicycle and the conventional tourer. If the mountain bike does no more than convince people that high gears and ultra-narrow tyres are not the best solution for cycle-touring then it will still have been a success.

Fig. 12 A mountain bike—low gears, fat tyres, flat bars,
wide clearances, long wheelbase, shallow frame angles.
(Photograph courtesy Muddy Fox)

THREE

THE SPECIALISED TOURING BICYCLE

In this lengthy chapter we look at the major components of a bicycle designed specifically for touring, of the type that can be ordered from one of the many small artisan cycle builders. This is likely to be expensive, but you *will* have exactly the machine you require. As a guide to cost, the price of a hand-built frame has, over the years, almost exactly matched the British national average gross weekly pay; the rest of the bicycle, depending on how elaborate it is, costs from the same again to perhaps twice as much. A hand-built frame—with periodic enamelling and reasonable treatment—should serve you for a good 30 years. However, Chapter 5 looks at bicycles down to a budget.

The frame

The frame is the essential skeleton of the bicycle—and its dimensions decide whether the bicycle can be made to fit you. The frame size mentioned in catalogues and specifications is the length of the seat tube, the one leading from the bottom bracket (where the chain-

Fig. 13 Naming of parts: **1** frame, *see figure 14 for details*; **2** saddle; **3** seat pillar; **4** rear brake; **5** bag carrier; **6** rear mudguard; **7** reflector; **8** rear wheel, tyre and rim; **9** spoke; **10** rear gear; **11** freewheel block mounted on rear hub; **12** chain; **13** and **14** chainrings; **15** crank; **16** toeclip with toestrap; **17** pedal; **18** mudflap; **19** tyre valve; **20** front hub; **21** front hub quick-release lever; **22** front brake mechanism; **23** brake lever; **24** brake cable; **25** handlebar bend; **26** handlebar stem; **27** gear lever; **28** pump; **29** bottle cage; **30** front gear mechanism

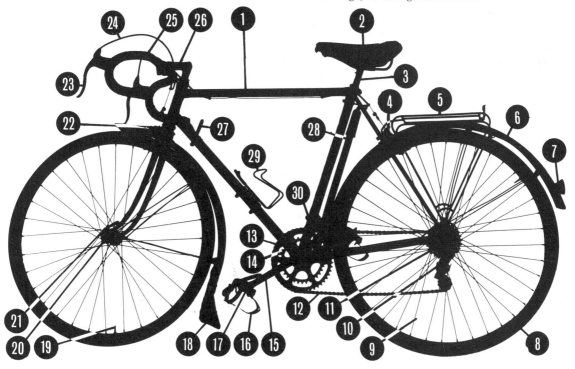

27

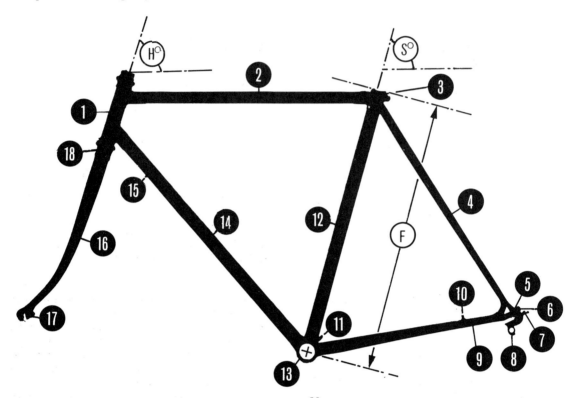

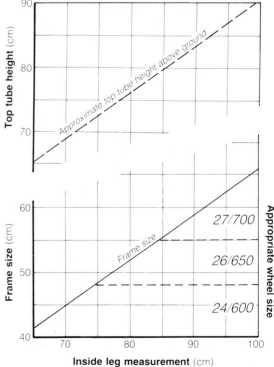

Fig. 14 The parts of the frame: **1** head tube; **2** top tube; **3** seat cluster (seat lug and clamp bolt); **4** seat stay; **5** rear fork end; **6** mudguard eye; **7** rear axle stop adjuster; **8** rear gear hanger; **9** seat stay; **10** rear gear cable stop; **11** tunnel for gear control cable wires; **12** seat tube; **13** bottom bracket shell; **14** down tube; **15** gear lever stop; **16** front fork blade; **17** front fork end incorporating mudguard eye; **18** fork crown. F is the quoted size of the frame, measured British fashion; H° and s° are the quoted head and seat angles respectively

wheel fits) towards the saddle. British frames usually progress in ½in steps—21, 21½, 22 and so on—although some makers, and of course those in other countries, now work entirely to metric measurements.

Note that in other countries, measurement at the top end may be made to the centre line of the top tube rather than the seat lug, giving a quoted size about 15mm or ½in less.

There is a relationship between various body measurements and correct frame size. Figure 15 shows the frame size which goes with a given full inside leg measurement—from the crutch to the ground, without shoes—over a wide range. Large or small feet for your height, or a long or short thigh in relation to your total leg length, may call for some adjustment. A good bespoke frame builder will take these and other measurements into account.

Fig. 16 The frame which is the basis of the touring bicycle shown in Fig. 11

Frame angles figure large in cyclists' technical talk; the illustration shows as a matter of record, where they are measured. Frame angles—which can affect steering, comfort and the general liveliness of the bicycle—should be left to the builder since they are two of the valuable variables allowing a frame to be made to the right size *horizontally* as well as vertically. This is important above all with small frames; by manipulating, particulary, the seat angle, the forward reach and the saddle position relative to the bottom bracket can be matched to the rider. (A common fault with mass-produced off-the-peg frames below about 20in (51cm) is that they are just 'cut-down' versions of bigger ones with top tubes that are far too long and seat tubes too far back.) Short top tube design is made easier by fitting smaller wheels to smaller frames. I have indicated on the graph what I consider appropriate sizes. Don't be persuaded to buy a frame which is too big. As well as having the right position you must be able to stand astride the top tube of your bicycle with your feet flat on the ground.

Fig. 15 How to determine the correct frame size for you. The lower solid line shows the appropriate frame size, measured British fashion, for a given full inside leg measurement. The upper broken line gives the approximate top tube height above the ground: note that it's always less than the inside leg measurement so that it is always possible to stand astride the bicycle. The marked ranges at lower right suggest appropriate wheel diameters for given frame sizes

Lightweight frames are constructed from seamless drawn tubing of special alloy steel, the best known of which is the British Reynolds 531, brazed into lugs at the points where the tubes join. The high strength of the alloy steel allows the tubes to be made quite thin—it's from this and not from any intrisinically lower density that the lightness derives.

The best tubes are thin in the middle and of thicker wall section—internally 'butted'—at the ends and points of higher stress. Although strong, the frame is a piece of precision engineering, which is reflected in the price. Don't knock it about. The gauge of the tube walls varies also with the type of tubing. This in turn governs the seat pillar diameter required; ask the builder to tell you the correct size. Steering column diameter is effectively standard.

It is worth having certain fittings brazed on for neatness and convenience when the frame is made. These include: a gear cable stop on the right-hand chainstay; gear cable guides or tunnels under the bottom bracket, for both front and rear gears; brake-cable guides on the top tube for the rear brake cable; if centre-pull brakes are fitted, a rear hanger behind the seat stays to take the cable end; gear lever bosses or a small stop for clip-on gear levers on the down tube; and tapped bosses on the down tube for a drinking bottle cage. Frame-fitting pumps which nestle between the top and down tubes have made brazed-on pump fittings unnecessary. For maximum strength and aesthetics, mudguard and carrier eyes should be incorporated into fork ends, and now that gear fittings on frames are standardised on the Campagnolo-originated 10mm fitting, a right-hand rear fork end incorporating the gear fixing hanger is also desirable.

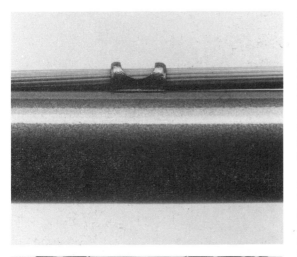

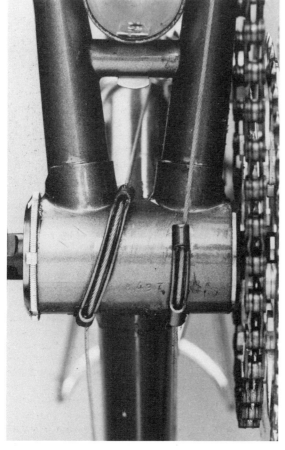

Fig. 17 Among the useful braze-ons when the frame is made: brake cable guides on top of the top tube and gear cable channels under the bottom bracket

In general it is best to stick to braze-ons which are standard fittings.

As well as body dimensions and wheel size, your frame builder will need to discuss the length of crank you intend to use, your shoe size and the fact that you mean to use the frame for touring, so that clearance can be adequately allowed for at the right points and the best bottom bracket height determined. Crank lengths are discussed further on in this chapter. The other factor affected by wheel size is the rear end clearance for the hub, to be discussed later.

No mention has been made so far about frames specifically for female riders—for the simple reason that most experienced women, like their male counterparts, have always used the universal design of 'diamond' frame. The open type of frame is rather susceptible to the twisting stresses it gets in anything other than very gentle riding, accentuated when the bicycle is loaded at the rear. If you prefer an open frame, a more rigid design is the popularly-called 'mixte' in which a pair of thinnish parallel tubes runs right through from the head to the rear fork end, bridged for stiffness.

Tyres and wheels

Two different types of **tyre** are used on bicycles. The 'tubular'—colloquially 'tub'—are used mainly for racing and are glued to a special crescent-shaped rim. They are, hardly surprisingly, tubular in cross-section, with the very light canvas (or even silk) part—properly known as the 'pocket'—sewn up along the base with a very thin latex tube inside. To repair them a strongly-stuck base tape, which protects the threads, has to be removed and a section of base stitching undone to reach the tube. Riders therefore usually carry spares. In view mainly of this need and tubulars' general fragility and liability to chafe on a laden bike, together with the difficulty of sticking a spare on by the roadside strongly enough for safety, they are not to be recommended for touring. You may hear claims of prodigious rides without a single puncture, but it's the nature of things that those who spend desperate evenings in hotel bedrooms repairing their punctured spares don't boast about it. For racing, tubs are fine; for touring, no. The same applies for the new generation of very light and narrow 'wired-on' tyres.

'Wired-on' tyres are the second type and probably more familiar. The outer cover has a wire, usually steel, built into its edges, which seat onto surfaces on the rim; a rubber or tough cloth rim tape covers the spoke heads or wells, and the air is retained in a separate inner tube.

Fashion in wheel sizes in Britain changes: up to the 1950s, 26in were the thing, then 27in took over, now the European 700c is in. The nomenclatures are confusing and arbitrary. About the only thing that can be easily defined with precision is the 'bead seat diameter'—the outside diameter of the rim measured to the little humps that the tyre wire sits on. The table below lists the commonest sizes and their colloquial equivalents.

Common British name	Bead seat diameter (mm)	Common continental name	Typical outside diameter of inflated tyre†	
			(mm)	(in)
$27 \times 1\frac{1}{4}$	630		698	27.48
700★	622	700c	686	27.00
$26 \times 1\frac{1}{4}$	597		663	26.10
$26 \times 1\frac{3}{8}$	590	650a	656	25.83
$26 \times 1\frac{1}{2}$	584	650b	650	25.60
	541	600a		
$24 \times 1\frac{3}{8}$	540		606	23.86

★because they have the same bead seat diameter as the largely obsolete British roadster size $28 \times 1\frac{5}{8}$, these are sometimes confusingly referred to abroad as 28in, even though they're smaller than 27s.

†for interest and for the record: actual measured values with roughly comparable tyres.

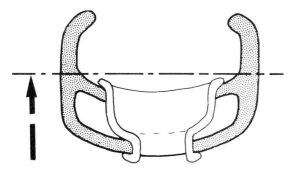

Fig. 18 Cross-section of one type of box-section rim showing, roughly, where the bead seat diameter is measured to. Other types of rim have more marked humps on which the tyre bead seats

Tyres of the same bead seat diameter can have different cross-sectional widths, expressed in Britain often in nominal inch fraction sizes or elsewhere in mm. Because common designations such as $27 \times 1\frac{1}{4}$ also defined rim sizes, problems arose with narrower or

Fig. 19 The writing on the (tyre) wall. *Left to right:* ETRTO size designation; colloquial size (in brackets); inflation recommendation.

fatter tyres on the same rim, leading to such absurdities as '$28 \times 1\frac{5}{8} \times 1\frac{1}{4}$'. European manufacturers now use an agreed European Tyre and Rim Technical Organisation (ETRTO) designation—marked on the walls of all tyres—combining the nominal inflated cross-section in mm and the actual bead seat sizes. So '$27 \times 1\frac{1}{4}$' becomes unambiguously ETRTO 32–630; narrower tyres for the same rims are now 25–630 or 28–630. Similarly '650×32B' becomes 32–584, '700×23c' is 23–622, and so on.

The tourist seeks a compromise between tyres that run easily, which means thin, and ones that are reliable and give some relief from road shocks. This compromise is best met by a tyre of 32mm section, certainly not less than 28mm, with a not-too-heavy but definite tread and thinly rubber-coated flexible walls—usually amber or showing the canvas colour. Even fatter ones, 37 or 40mm, can be better on rough roads. Except in mud or above a certain depth of snow, tread pattern has less effect on roadholding than rubber composition and inflation. Suitable tyres are Michelin's Sports or High Speed or their foldable Hi-Lite which has a flexible plastic 'wire'. There are many others similar— but be wary of some non-Japanese Far Eastern tyres: some of the size variations are too great to allow proper mounting on the rim.

The size of wheel and tyre should properly be determind by frame size; below about a $21\frac{1}{2}$in (55cm) frame size there is a strong case for using 26in or 650 tyres, below 19in (48cm) for using 600 or 24in. If you expect to travel widely in Europe, tyres for 700C, 650B or 650A are more readily available in most places than 27 or $26 \times 1\frac{1}{4}$. In Britain $27 \times 1\frac{1}{4}$, 700C and $26 \times 1\frac{1}{4}$ or $1\frac{3}{8}$ are relatively easy to find, although moderately light tyres in the latter two sizes are not too plentiful off the shelf, nor wider-section 700C.

The resistance of tyres to wear can be considerably extended by buying them well before they are needed and allowing them to 'mature' for a year or two in darkness and at normal room temperatures. Rear tyres wear more rapidly than front ones, so it is reasonable to change them round after a time. Remember, though that the front tyre is the key one in control: never fit a dubious tyre to the front wheel.

Inner tubes are of two types—butyl (black) and natural rubber (red or 'rubber-coloured'). Butyl tubes, now by far the commonest, retain their pressure when unpunctured almost indefinitely but take longer to repair (which makes it worth carrying a spare or two: they don't take up much space). The valve most commonly used on lightweight wheels is the 'Presta' or high-pressure. It has a narrow body with a small screw-down plunger; it needs a suitable pump connector or adapter with enough bored-out depth to clear the plunger when unscrewed. The car-type Schräder

Fig. 21 Luxury for home use, particularly if there's more than one bicycle in the house: the 'track' pump with pressure gauge

valve is not generally used for British lightweight cycles, although some imported models may have them. The old Woods valve, usually used on roadster bicycles, is the one with valve rubber or a small insert and needs an 8mm hole in the rim.

Although inner tubes are made in specific diameters they are not as critical as outer covers; 700C and 27 are served by the same tube, for example. You can with care use a 27in tube in a 26in tyre, but it's less easy the other way round.

European tyres now have their recommended inflation pressure marked on the wall with all the other figures; otherwise 4.5 atmospheres (about 70psi) is a good starting point. You can get small pressure gauges to check Presta-valved tyres (real luxury—for home use, not for carrying with you—is a 'track' pump with a built-in gauge and easy inflation) but your thumb will soon gain the experience needed to assess the right pressure pretty accurately.

Fig. 20 *From left to right:* Schräder, Woods and Presta valves. Before air can be released or the tyre pumped up, the small knurled locking nut of the Presta valve must be unscrewed to its limit *(extreme right)*. It's then worth giving a quick dab with the finger on this nut to make sure that the plunger is free to move before trying to pump the tyre up. For touring use the plastic caps supplied to keep dirt out of the valve

Fig. 22 A modern quick-release hub

Fig. 23 How a quick-release hub works. The base of the locking lever carries a cam which, when the lever is operated, pulls the adjustable fixing A inwards on a skewer which passes through the hollow axle. In its open or unlocked position *(left)* there is clearance for the hub to be removed or inserted *(arrowed)*. When locked *(right)*, the hub is clamped in. A should be adjusted in the unlocked position until moving the lever to the locked position shown holds the wheel firmly

Wheels and tyres are about the easiest thing to change on a bicycle—within the range of the brake adjustment—so it's not a once-and-for-all decision. It's reasonable, even desirable, to have different wheels for different purposes: summer and winter, or home and abroad.

The wheel itself looks at first sight like a fairly complex piece of wire knitting. A closer look reveals that it is an ingenious piece of metallic applied geometry, said to have one of the highest strength/weight ratios known. It is made up from three components: a central hub, wire spokes and a rim.

All but the cheapest modern **hubs** are made of aluminium alloy forgings with steel axles and bearings. The hub flanges—which have holes into which the heads of the spokes fit—can be either small (about 48–52mm) or large (about 72–76mm) diameter. In theory a small-flange hub builds up into a slightly more flexible and resilient wheel; this is probably far more influenced by the style and tension of spoking and by the type of rim. I would nevertheless suggest small-flange hubs for touring wheels. The flanges must be thick enough for the bent portion of the spoke to have an adequate seating.

The rear hub has a threaded portion next to the flange on one or both sides for the freewheel or other sprocket. The standard British threading is $1\frac{3}{8}$in × 24TPI. On hubs intended for multiple freewheels this threading covers a length of about 8–9mm.

Hubs are held in the frame in two ways: either by a hexagonal nut with a built-in serrated washer ('track nuts') or by a lever-operated 'quick-release' cam mechanism. Except for street parking, quick-release hubs have several advantages. They make wheel removal easy for puncture repair, for travelling by air or in a car with limited boot space, for clearing out mud or leaves, or for attending the brakes and gears. Quick-

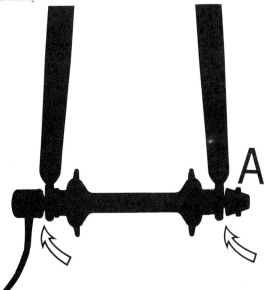

release axles are hollow to take the skewer of the cam mechanism. They are usually made of higher-quality steel and are stronger than many solid axles.

The usual width for a front hub—measured to the outside of the locknuts—is 100mm, and of a rear hub 120mm (for standard 5-speed freewheeel) or 126mm (for a 6-speed).

The standard for hubs is set by the Italian firm Camagnolo, as is—for the Record model—the top price. Such has been the influence of this company on the last 30 years of component design that nearly every other manufacturer produces Campagnolo look-alikes. (When the Great History of Cycling comes to be written, Campagnolo's influence in imposing *de facto* standard sizes on the industry may be revealed as their finest acheivement.) My recommendation in hubs is their less-expensive Nuovo Tipo type in its small-flange quick-release 5-speed guise. Shimano, Sun Tour, Zeus, Mavic, to name only a few, produce comparable models.

Fig. 24 Sections of wheels showing *(left to right/top to bottom)*: radial ('o-cross', in effect), 2-cross, 3-cross and 4-cross spoking. For clarity spokes on only one side of the wheel are shown. Note that on the 4-cross example, one of the crossings occurs before the spokes have reached the outside of the hub flange. It is this potential crossing of spokes over the actual heads of adjacent ones that limits the use of 4-cross spoking—and makes higher numbers impossible

Spokes are either zinc-coated (rather misleadingly called 'rustless'), chromium-plated or made of stainless steel. There seems to be a lot of variation in quality in stainless, while chromed ones are very pretty to begin with but soon rust where they fret at the crossings.

The usual thickness for solo bicycle spokes now seems to be 14SWG (2.00mm), sometimes lightened with a thinner central section (16SWG, 1.63mm) where the stresses are less ('double butted' like the frame tubes but external). Thicker ones, 13SWG (2.24mm) or even 12SWG (2.64mm) can be used for tandems or heavy-duty wheels; hub flanges and, sometimes, rims do have to be drilled out to take them.

The number of spokes varies. British practice used to be 32 in the front wheel, 40 in the rear; other countries had 36 in both. Generally 36/36 hubs and, particularly, rims are easier to find and replace so this combination is best for normal use. You might prefer the (very slight) extra strength of a 40 rear if you are heavily built or expect to be heavily laden. Lighter wheels for racing use combinations of 24, 28 or 32.

There are various patterns of spoking which can be used in a wheel, defined by the number of times a spoke crosses on its way from the hub to the rim. Theoretically at least, more crossings lead to a more resilient

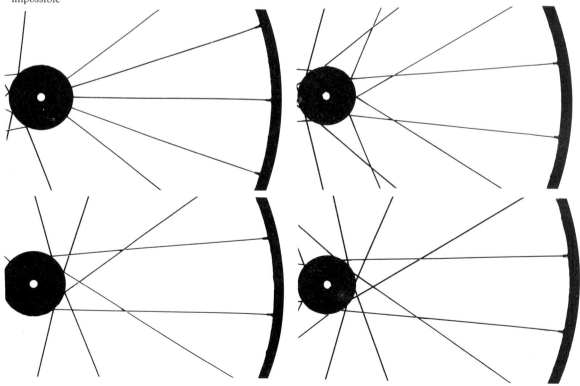

Fig. 25 The 26mm wide and very rigid Mavic Module 4 rim, the widest of this firm's series of box-section extruded rims, made in a range of diameters. This width is suitable for tyres of 32mm section upwards. Good quality rims of this type are counterbalanced at the mechanical joint for the weight of the valve: the old tale about a good wheel rotating under the weight of its own valve just doesn't apply to a *really* good one. This type of rim needs a sturdy rim tape to cover the spoke wells, as shown here

wheel, although the tension to which they are tightened may have more effect. For a basic touring wheel I would recommend 3-cross for small-flange 36-spoke wheels.

The final component is the **rim**. The best rims are, like hubs, in aluminium alloy, rolled from shaped extrusions and welded into a circle or mechanically jointed. The best have a box section with the spoke holes reinforced with single or double steel eyelets. Steel rims are heavier, if stronger, with poorer wet braking. The width of the rim should match the tyre reasonably well: too narrow a rim and you may have inner tube puncture problems and tyre wall chafing;

too wide and the tyre is spread, leading to an uncomfortable ride and uncertain handling. Broadly speaking 19 or 20mm rims (measured externally) suit 19–23mm tyres, 22mm rims suit 23–28 and some 32mm tyres, 26mm rims suit 32mm and fatter tyres. You must use a suitable rim tape to cover the spoke wells, particularly with rims of this type. The most comprehensive rim range is made by the French firm Mavic; other good ones are Wolber Super Champion, also French, and the Italian Nisi. The Swiss/Belgian company Weinmann make a wide range of sizes in a simpler solid section; since they are not eyeletted, these Weinmann and Nisi rims can be drilled for larger spoke nipples than 14swg. Super Champion, Weinmann and Nisi make rims in 541mm and some smaller sizes.

Calculating spoke length—
a mathematical interlude

Calculating spoke length is an interesting mathematical exercise involving the Cosine Rule and Pythagoras' Theorem. The following variables need to be taken into consideration:

D = inside the diameter of rim
d = spoke hole pitch circle diameter on hub
N = number of spokes
n = number of spoke crossings
f = hub flange separation
s = lateral spoke hole separation or rims with staggered hole pattern
δ = dishing (deviation of rim from centre line between hub flanges for asymmetrical wheels for multiple freewheels)
e = depth spoke penetrates into nipple, measured from the outer rim surface

The angle $\dfrac{720n}{N}$ is expressed in degrees; it would be $\dfrac{4\pi n}{N}$ if it were in radians. This gives the magnificent expression for spoke length L:

$$L = \tfrac{1}{2}[D^2 + d^2 - 2dD\cos\left(\frac{720n}{N}\right) + (f - s \pm 2\delta)^2]^{\frac{1}{2}} + e$$

However, in practice, the effect of f, s and δ are negligible now that rear wheels are much less dished than they used to be (and given that many stockists have spokes only to the nearest 3mm or $\frac{1}{8}$in). A typical value of e is 5mm for eyeletted rims, otherwise 4mm. In addition there are not many practical values of n/N, so that if we assign a value A to the function $2\cos\left(\dfrac{720n}{N}\right)$ for these combinations, the expression simplifies to

$$L = \tfrac{1}{2}[D^2 + d^2 - AdD]^{\frac{1}{2}} + 5$$

where A has the following values: 32-hole, 3-cross, $A = 0.766$; 36-hole, 3-cross, $A = 1.000$; 36-hole, 4-cross, $A = 0.348$; 40-hole, 3-cross, $A = 1.176$; 40-hole, 4-cross, $A = 0.618$. D and d are both very simple to measure (see the illustration) but the following are typical values:

D (in mm)

$27 \times 1\frac{1}{4}$: Weinmann Alesa $D = 615$; Super Champion 58 $D = 613$;
700c: Weinmann Alesa $D = 608$; Mavic $D = 608$;
$26 \times 1\frac{1}{4}$: Weinmann Alesa $D = 584$; 650B: $D = 565$.

d (also in mm)

Campagnolo small-flange   front $d = 40$; rear $d = 44.5$
Campagnolo large-flange   front $d = 63$; rear $d = 63$.

(most Campagnolo-style hubs by other makers have similar dimensions).
For other values of n/N or e:

$$L = \tfrac{1}{2}\left[D^2 + d^2 - 2dD\cos\left(\frac{720n}{N}\right)\right]^{\frac{1}{2}} + e$$

Gears and gearing

Gears and gearing is a contentious subject: a source of endless discussion, argument and disagreement. However, the suggestions made here embody a system that has been found to work well both with experienced riders and with novices (who perhaps have the advantage of not having to unlearn).

In Chapter 1 we saw that reasonable figure for the lowest road speed was about 7kph (4.5mph) and that this appears, from observation, to demand a pedalling rate of around 55rpm. By 20kph (say 12mph) a comfortable cadence becomes about 70rpm. For a touring cyclist a reasonable top speed while still pedalling—up to the point where you'd naturally freewheel—is probably about 32kph (20mph). At this speed 90rpm or so feels right.

At 55rpm at 7kph, each turn of the pedals would take the rider about 2.1m; 90rpm at 32kph, 5.9m. Intermediate speeds call for intermediate values: 70rpm at 20kph needs 4.8m, for example. We can thus construct a graph relating speed to distance covered per turn of the pedals (Fig. 27).

Fig. 26

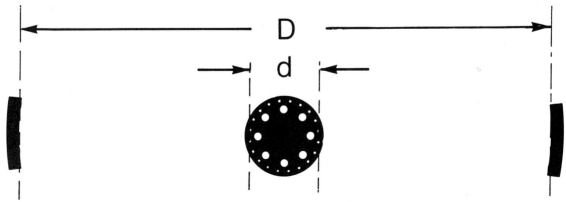

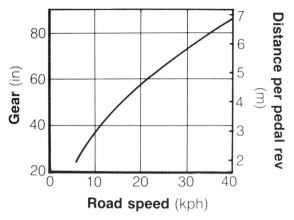

Fig. 27 Gear sizes—on the left in inches on the British system, on the right in metres travelled per pedal turn—as a function of road speed. This curve is derived from the graph in Fig. 2 which is based on observation of experienced riders

In a rational world gears would be expressed in this way, as metres/pedal rev (and indeed they are in France). But this simple notion lacks the sense of history that Britons demand. British gears are instead given as the diameter of wheel in inches a direct-drive ungeared bicycle would need to travel the same distance. The fact that there hasn't actually been a direct-drive bicycle since the high Ordinary ('Penny Farthing') was superseded in the 1880s does nothing to

Fig. 28 Big chainring + small sprocket = high gear
Small chainring + big sprocket = low gear

shake the system. However, the figures are easy ones to remember, provided you don't complicate matters by using all the decimal places your calculator offers. Our 2.1m turns out to be 26in, 4.8m to be 60in, and 5.9m to be 74in. So, rounding off, a range of 25 to 75in would appear to cover most requirements.

Nearly all off-the-peg bicycles are sold with higher gear ratios than this, often up to 100in or more. Big gears have their uses in competition—I have made good use of a 108in gear in road races (combined with pedalling rates in the 100–110 range)—but I have never found anything higher than 75 to be of any appreciable use when touring.

The different gear ratios are obtained by using front chainwheels and rear freewheel sprockets of different size, expressed as the number of teeth each has on its circumference. Chainwheels in common use range from 24 teeth up to about 54, freewheel sprockets from 12 to 34. Both series have some gaps.

Variable gears are achieved by having usually five or six freewheel sprockets mounted side-by-side on the rear wheel hub and one, two or three chainwheels side-by-side and connected to the pedal cranks. Derailleur gear mechanisms (so-called because they were first popularised in France and because they 'derail' the

Fig. 29 How a derailleur gear works. The lever has been moved to change up and the parallelogram and cage are moving outwards under the force of the spring, with the jockey pulley pulling the chain from the bottom (big) sprocket of the freewheel onto the next one

Fig. 30 How a derailleur works, again. The spring-loaded cage and the jockey pulleys take up the slack in the chain on different gears. Note how the slanting gear parallelogram arm moves the top jockey pulley close to the appropriate sprocket—an aid to precise gear changing

chain from sprocket to sprocket) move the chain as required and take up the inevitable slack. The theoretical number of different gears available is the number of chainwheels used multiplied by the number of freewheel sprockets (e.g. $2 \times 5 = 10$), but in practice the chain does not run well in extreme crossovers: particularly from the innermost chainring to the outermost sprocket.

The gear ratio in inches is given by the expression

$$\frac{\text{Number of teeth on chainwheel} \times \text{diameter of rear wheel (in)}}{\text{number of teeth on sprocket}}$$

Thus a 36-tooth chainring with an 18-sprocket gives, with a 27in wheel, a gear of $36 \times 27/18 = 54$. (There's no real point in quoting gears any more precisely than to the nearest inch.) With the now ubiquitous pocket calculator this is a very simple calculation. It is easier to carry out the multiplication stage first, store the result, then recall it and divide by each of the sprocket sizes in turn.

You could, given the available sizes of components, more or less cover the range 25 to 75 with a single chainring (something like a 34T ring with 12–15–18–22–28–34 freewheel) but there are several disadvantages. First is that the changes between adjacent gears are very large, something like 25 per cent, which can be very disconcerting. Change down and it feels as though you're pedalling on air; change up and it feels as though something's jammed. The other disadvantages are mechanical: the actual jump that the chain has to make is very large so that changing is uncertain and noisy, the freewheel is large and heavy and a special gear mechanism is needed to clear the very large freewheel sprocket.

I would suggest, therefore, even for the novice, choosing the triple chainwheel with a 5- or narrow 6-speed freewheel. The system has quite small differences between freewheel sprockets (about 10–12 per cent) and fairly small ones between the chainrings (18 and 28 per cent—quite close for chainrings). In practical use most of the changes are made on the rear gear; the big chainring is used mainly on easy roads at speeds above about 15kph, the middle ring on undulat-

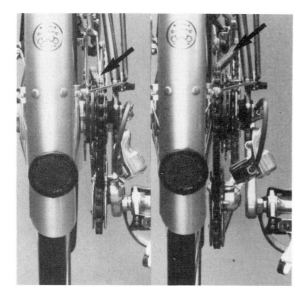

Fig. 31 Why you can't use the extreme 'crossover' gears satisfactorily. On the inside chainring and next-to-top rear sprocket *(left)* the chain still runs reasonably straight; on the big ring and bottom sprocket *(right)* it is being pulled at too great an angle. On the opposite extreme, smallest ring and top sprocket, the chain may also touch the middle chainring

ing roads at speeds from about 10 to 20kph and the bottom one for the tough ones, below about 11kph. In other words, you will be using the system almost as three separate sets of four or five fairly close-ratio gears: an 'easy' set, a 'medium' set and a 'hard' set, selected according to the conditions. Once the gears are fitted forget the numbers and change when your legs tell you that you need to. It's all much less complex in use than it may sound; see Chapter 14.

The suggestion, then, for 27in or 700c wheels, is a combination of 44–36–26 chainwheels with 16–18–20–23–27 or 15–17–19–21–23–26 freewheels. You could try a 15–17–19–21–24–28 as an alternative to give a slightly lower bottom gear if you choose.

For 26in or 650A or 650B wheels, I would suggest 46–38–28 chainwheels with the 16–18–20–23–27 5-speed freewheel or again the 44–36–26 with 15–17–19–21–23–26.

To give roughly the same gear range with 600 (24in) wheels, use 44–37–28 chainwheels with a 14–16–18–21–24 freewheel. Specific makes of freewheel are suggested below.

For the record the following tables give you the gear ratios obtained with the various combinations. The circled ones are the extreme crossovers which are not normally usable.

Gear ratios for a 24in wheel

No of chainwheel teeth	No of freewheel teeth				
	14	16	18	21	24
44	75	66	59	50	(44)
37	63	56	49	42	37
28	(48)	42	37	32	28

Gear ratios for a 26in wheel
5-SPEED FREEWHEEL

No of chainwheel teeth	No of freewheel teeth				
	16	18	20	23	27
46	75	66	60	52	(44)
38	62	55	49	43	37
28	(46)	40	36	32	27

6-SPEED FREEWHEEL

No of chainwheel teeth	No of freewheel teeth					
	15	17	19	21	23	26
44	76	67	60	54	50	(44)
36	62	55	49	45	41	36
26	(45)	40	36	32	29	26

With comparable tyres, 650B wheels give gears about 2 per cent lower and 650A 1 per cent lower—a difference hardly significant.

Gear ratios for a 27in wheel
5-SPEED FREEWHEEL

No of chainwheel teeth	No of freewheel teeth				
	16	18	20	23	27
44	74	66	59	52	(44)
36	61	54	49	42	36
26	(44)	39	35	31	26

6-SPEED FREEWHEEL

No of chainwheel teeth	No of freewheel teeth						or		
	15	17	19	21	23	26		24	28
44	77	70	63	57	52	(46)		50	(42)
36	65	57	51	46	42	37		41	35
26	47	(41)	37	33	31	27		29	25

700c wheels give gears effectively about 1 per cent lower, assuming comparable types; the difference is again almost negligible.

Multiple **freewheels** are commonly available with five, six and seven sprockets. All take the $\frac{1}{2} \times \frac{3}{32}$in (12.7 × 2.38mm) size of chain (the actual sprocket thickness is 2.0mm). However, to cram more and more sprockets in, the width of the spacers between sprockets has been reduced by about 0.8mm relative to standard freewheels to allow 'narrow' or 'compact' freewheels to be introduced. These need a special chain, with flush bearing pins: suitable makes are Sedisport, Sun Tour Ultra-6 or Superbe and Regina CXS. A 'compact' 6-speed is only about 2mm wider than a standard 5, and both fit the 120mm overall width rear hub. A 'compact' 7 or standard 6 requires the 126mm rear hub. I would advise keeping to the 'compact' 6 or standard 5, since others are more offset, calling for more wheel 'dishing' with the most heavily loaded bearing further from the support of the frame. Both features introduce a small but definite increase in the chances of spoke or axle breakage, particularly on a laden bicycle.

Only the Japanese Sun Tour Perfect and the Italian Regina 5-speed models permit the use of a 16T top sprocket in conjuction with an 18T as the next. Only Sun Tour has a 27T in the range but, oddly, no 25T in this fitting; Regina has 25T, 26T and 28T. In narrow 6-speed models only the French Maillard Compact allows a 15T–17T top pair combination, although hybrids can be constructed. On Sun Tour and Maillard freewheels the smaller sprockets screw onto the freewheel body and hold the larger ones in place; the latter slide on to splines on the freewheel body. On Regina freewheels the smaller three sprockets screw on normally from the front and the larger two, with a left-hand thread, from the back. Sprockets are rarely interchangeable between different makes. All freewheels require a simple tool—usually specific to that make—to remove them undamaged from the hub.

Gear mechanisms have the task of shifting the chain from sprocket to sprocket or chainwheel to chainwheel.

Fig. 32 The front gear is a simple cage which shifts the chain from ring to ring

All modern **rear gear mechanisms** have a flexible parallelogram-shaped arm which carries a spring-loaded cage with two tensioning or 'jockey' pulleys. The upper jockey pulley pushes or pulls the chain from one sprocket to the next; the lower one moves forwards and back under the influence of the sprung cage to take up the slack in the chain. In the best designs the parallelogram arm is aligned and the cage axis chosen in such a way that the cage moves down as it moves in, following the approximate line of the sprockets. The closer the top jockey pulley remains to the bottom of the sprockets, the more rapid and positive the gear change. The 'capacity' of the gear is often quoted as a certain number of teeth, the total of the differences between the largest and smallest chainrings and sprockets, defining the ability of the gear to take up the slack in the chain. In the case of the gear ratios I have suggested the required capacity is about 28T, well within the capacity of the usual compact racing-style gear; there is no need to have the less elegant long-arm versions.

The travel in towards the spokes and out towards the frame is limited by screw-adjusting stops. Suitable rear mechanisms include the Japanese Sun Tour Cyclone II and ARX and the Shimano new 600EX.

Front mechanisms incorporate no chain tensioning system. Most consist simply of a curved cage though which the chain passes and in which pushes the chain sideways until it engages with the next chainring. Most front mechanisms will cope with the chainring sizes I suggest. Suitable models are again Sun Tour Cyclone II and Simano New 600EX. The Italian Campagnolo Gran Sport and Record also work well.

Gear control levers may be fitted either side of the frame down tube, the usual position, on the ends of the handlebars, on the handlebar stem or, by using levers originally designed for 'off-road' bicycles, on a suitable part of the handlebar bend. I would recommend, at least to begin with, the common down-tube position, which offers the least complicated and most direct cable run. Gears sold as sets—or 'ensembles' as the trade likes to say—usually come complete with down-tube fittings. In all cases the right-hand lever controls the rear gear and the left-hand the front. All the rear gears have the top gear position at the furthest forward point of the level travel and the bottom gear at the back. All the front gears recommended work in the opposite direction—forward for the smallest ring and lowest gear and backwards for the largest.

Cranks, chainwheel and pedals

Cranks for lightweight bicycles are made of aluminium alloy and use a special axle with tapered square ends. They are held in position by bolts screwing into tapped holes in the ends of the axle. Most types have their own individual fitting and special tools are required—and supplied—for each. They are particularly necessary for removal. The **chainrings** are bolted to the cranks in a variety of ways, although there appears to be some standardisation. The most versatile are the 5-pin fixings used by the French manufacturers Stronglight and TA and now adopted by some Japanese makers such as Sakae Ringyo (SR) and Sugino. The tourist needs to have available very small front chainrings— the TA or Stronglight 49D 5-pin fixing allows this, when used together with TA Cyclotouriste rings, or the Stronglight 99/100 or SR Custom 5 fitting. The gearing system I advocate uses three chainrings and requires an intermediate ring with 36 or 38 teeth. Some makes, although taking a very small innermost ring, will not go below 42T as the intermediate. Different lengths of bottom bracket axle are available for different chainring configurations. Triple chainsets with 28 or 26T inside rings can usually be used with 'long double' 123mm axles.

It is possible to make a similar, although less precise, correlation between inside leg length and **crank** length in the way that we did for frame size. Foot size and thigh to inside leg ratios may alter choice slightly.

Fig. 33 The pedal and toeclip assembly. These track-type pedals are better for wide feet than the quill types. Note the 'R' on the spanner flat *(right)* showing that it is a right-hand pedal

Most makes of crank are available in lengths of 175mm (nominally 7in), 170mm ($6\frac{3}{4}$in) and 165mm ($6\frac{1}{2}$in); TA ones are imported in 11 different lengths from 150mm (6in) to 185mm ($7\frac{1}{4}$in).

Inside leg measurement (cm)	Corresponding frame size (cm	Appropriate crank length (cm)
65–74	42–48	150
71–78	46–51	160
74–83	84–54	165
80–92	52–60	170
90–	59–	175

Pedals are again one of your personal contacts with the machine and need to be chosen with some care. Price is generally an indication of the quality of construction. Only all-metal pedals are considered here, as it is assumed that you will eventually fit toeclops and straps. Check, when wearing the shoes to be worn for cycling, that there is enough width of pedal to support the foot and still allow clearance between the foot and the crank, with room for a strap. The 'track' versions are generally better for touring; the Japanese SR and KKT track models are relatively inexpensive. Campagnolo ones are superb but about three times the price. The French Lyotard ones are less elegant but their range includes some very wide ones—and some double-sided ones which are desirable for urban riding. Avoid the cheapest steel pedals which have plain sintered bearings.

·Pedals screw into the ends of the cranks, the right-hand one with a right-hand thread, the left-hand with a left-hand thread. There is a standard thread for British use, $\frac{9}{16}$in × 20TPI. Never attempt to force a pedal into a thread it doesn't want to fit in; check that the pedal is at right-angles to the crank, and that it is indeed a right-hand pedal that you are trying to fit to a right-hand crank, or left to left! If necessary get the shop to clean out the crank thread with a tap. Some pedals are made with longer threads (about 13mm as against the usual 9mm) for use with thick alloy cranks: they are too long for Campagnolo and similar cranks.

Toeclips bolt onto the front plate of the pedal (in the case of single-sided pedals which can be used only one way up, when the pedal is the right way round); some have specially placed holes, ready tapped for the fixing bolts. The most universally used make of clip is the French AFA Christophe, and all sizes from other manufacturers correspond with the Christophe sizes. For shoe sizes up to British 5 (continental 38) 'D' or short toeclips are appropriate: from sizes $5\frac{1}{2}$ to 8 (39–42) medium; and from 9 (43) upwards, long. Above about $10\frac{1}{2}$ (45) you may need to put a packing piece (metal strip or plywood) between the long clip and the front pedal plate.

The clip determines the fore-and-aft positioning of the foot, but it has also the job of supporting the strap which holds the foot onto the pedal. These special **toe-straps** have a quick-release buckle which allows a wide range of close adjustment. It is essential that these buckles should be mounted the right way round so that a single flick of the finger loosens the strap when necessary. Toe-straps have many other applications as well, when a strong or adjustable fixing is needed.

Handlebars and stems

There is a huge variety of **handlebar shapes** on the market. Probably the best for touring is a squarish shape with a relatively modest drop, say 13 or 14cm (a little over 5in) and perhaps 10cm (4in) of forward reach. They are usually available in widths from 38cm upwards (in 2cm steps) from many different makers. This shape gives two comfortable 'on the tops' positions. The material is an aluminium alloy, this time drawn rather than forged. The standard diameter is 23.8mm ($\frac{15}{16}$in) with the centre part bulged or with a

Fig. 34 Modern handlebar stems have neat allen-key clamp and expander bolts. These Cinelli bars mate well with the TTT stem: both are from the same country, Italy. It is inadvisable to mix bar and stems from different countries

ferrule where it is gripped by the stem. There are variations in the bulged size: it is best to use bends and stems from the same manufacture, or at least from the same country.

The best type of handlebar **stem** is also in aluminium alloy and of the general shape of the one shown in Fig. 34. The lower part fits quite snugly into the steering or fork column of the frame. It is tightened by means of an allen-key socket-head bolt recessed into the top of the stem. This pulls up an 'expander' cone or wedge against the bottom of the stem and forces the latter outwards to grip the inside of the steering column. To loosen a stem you first have to loosen the expander bolt by a few turns and then tap it gently down to free the cone or wedge. The grip for the handlebar bend is also tightened by an allen-key bolt.

The length of the forward extension of the stem plays a key part in getting your position right (Chapter 4). Stems are available from about 40mm extension upwards to 140 or 150mm—measured from centre line of handlebar bend clamp to centre line of expander.

The most comprehensive range, although quite expensive, is made by the Italian firm Cinelli, the standard-setters. Cinelli 64 bends are quite a pleasant shape and have a slightly shorter reach then some, which may make them better for small riders. The

Fig. 35 The Mafac Racer is an example of a centre-pull brake

Japanese SR range is a good deal cheaper and includes shorter stem extensions; their Road Champion bend is quite a good touring model. There are many other makes: it is difficult to describe bend shapes exactly, and the best thing is to compare them side-by-side in the shop.

Brakes

There are two principal types of brake, again usually made in a forged aluminium alloy. The first, the **side-pull**, uses a type of scissor action to pull the two brake blocks in to grip the rim. There are many makes. There can be problems in centering some brakes of this kind so that neither brake block touches the rim when the brake is not being applied. Because touring brakes have to clear mudguards and substantial tyres, the leverage offered by side-pull brakes with the long arms

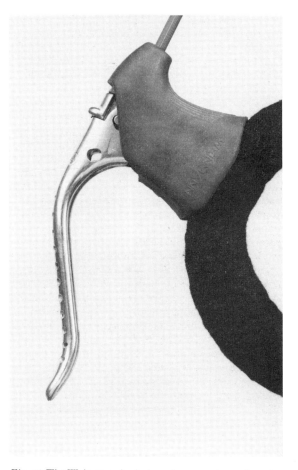

Fig. 36 The Weinmann brake lever incorporates a safe and fool-proof quick-release to allow wheels to be taken out past the brake blocks with ease. This lever, among others, has a short reach, making it suitable for small hands

necessary can make them less effective than the close-clearance racing versions and the centre-pull types.

The **centre-pull** brake is made in two forms, with brake-arm pivots on a central plate which bolts on to the fork crown or rear bridge, or with the pivots brazed on to the frame. In either type, the single wire from the brake lever is clamped to a small triangular cable guide. When the brake is applied both blocks move inwards with a considerable leverage—in the brazed-on version irrespective of mudguard or other clearance. The arms are independently mounted and sprung and centering is accomplished by adjusting the fixing plate or the individual brake block mountings. Centre-pull brakes are generally more lightly sprung than side-pulls and, despite a slight feeling of sponginess, are vey effective. The brazed-on version does not, however, allow major changes of mind on wheel size later. I would recommend Mafac, Weinmann or Dia-Compe centre-pulls; Mafac Criterium and Dia-Compe NGC 982 are suitable brazed-on versions.

Nearly all **brake levers** are similar in concept and most can be fitted with moulded rubber sleeves on the hood part to make comfortable hand rests. There is quite a variation in the reach needed to operate different levers. You should be able to crook the lever in the first joint of the middle two or three fingers, bending the second joint to apply the brake.

One recent type of lever should be guarded against: the horizontal extension levers frequently fitted to semi-lightweight bicycles. These, in theory at least, allow the brakes to be operated with the hands in the transverse 'on-the-tops' position. Just at the point where you need to exert maximum pull, however, with most handlebars bend shapes it is necessary to ease the lever forward or even away from the bar, a far from instinctive movement. The leverage is rather less than that available from the conventional lever, and they can interfere with front bag fitting; in addition you cannot fit brake hood rubbers. Better to learn to apply conventional levers from the top, as demonstrated in Chapter 14.

Another recent type of lever, developed originally as an 'aerodynamic' accessory for racing, might be worth consideration. These are of conventional shape but the cables pass backwards along or through the bar. This leaves the whole top area of the handlebars free of cables, which could be advantageous when a front bag or map carrier is used. A suitable lever is the Dia-Compe AGC 250H.

Saddles and seat pillars

The most comfortable saddles in practice are ones without apparent springing and with the top mounted on two stout wires or a Y-shaped frame. Saddle tops are made of two materials: thick leather, or plastic, with or without leather covering.

Before it achieves its true comfort, a **leather saddle** requires a period of breaking-in to mould it to your shape. The process is aided by dressing the saddle top in moderation with neatsfoot or castor oils. A well broken-in personally-shaped leather saddle is a joy to ride and ultimately the best—but you have to work to achieve it. Leather saddles should be protected from the wet as far as possible. Of current makes the British Brooks Professional (now also in a shorter wider-back version dubbed s or 'Lady') is probably the best. These models do not have saddlebag loops.

Plastic saddles—usually nylon—can be plain or covered with various types of leather, padded or

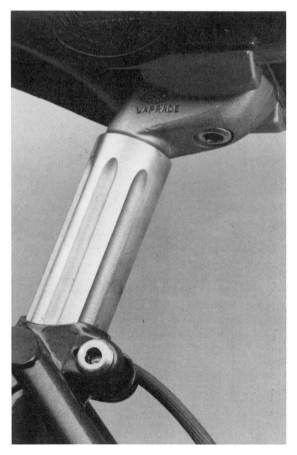

Fig. 37 A common type of seat pillar in which the saddle sits in a cast cradle adjustable for slope and fixed by the socket-head bolt

unpadded. Nylon can be moulded to a near-ideal resilience and some of the cheapest and plainest can be very comfortable. The Italians are masters of this trade and the Cinelli/Unica No. 55 plain model, being unaffected by wet, is very suitable for an everyday bicycle that may have to stand out in all weathers. These and the covered versions can be very comfortable from the start—but check carefully that the back part is wide enough: some racing ones are quite narrow; and some cheap ones are appallingly hard.

The saddle is fitted to a seat or **saddle pillar** or post. Most modern ones have an aluminium alloy cradle which grips the saddle wires and is adjustable for fore-and-aft position and for angle. These include Laprade (French), SR and Strong (Japanese) and Campagnolo. The part that fits into the frame seat tube can range in diameter from 25.0 to 27.4mm and must match the seat tube, sliding in smoothly without much play. The commonest diameters are 26.4, 26.8 and 27.2mm.

FOUR

FINAL ADJUSTMENTS

Riding position

We have already seen how frame size choice is governed by leg length. The graph on page 28 is based on allowing a both practical and aesthetic length of seat pillar to show above the frame when the position is right: if it *looks* right and comfortable, then it probably *is* right and comfortable.

The pedal position—determined by the frame bottom bracket position—is irrevocably fixed. The only variable is crank length, which has already been settled. so, any adjustments must be made to saddle and handlebar, saddle first, since this is fundamental to comfort.

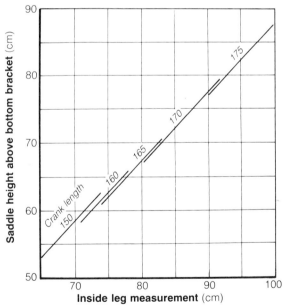

Fig. 38 The 'sat-on' surface of the saddle should be placed at the height shown—for the appropriate inside leg measurement and crank length—above the bottom bracket. This height is measured from the bracket centre along the line of the seat tube and is no more than a starting point. You may have to alter it to satisfy the positioning requirements on the next few pages and Fig. 39

Begin by raising or lowering the saddle pillar, by loosening the clamping bolt on the frame, until the distance from the sat-on part of the saddle top to the pedal axis when the crank is down and in line with the seat tube is about 5 per cent longer than your inside leg measurement. It's easier to measure it as saddle to bottom bracket centre, making allowance for crank length (see graph), but is only a starting point.

Now comes the fiddling part, best carried out with someone else as helper, measurer and observer. First, sit on the saddle, wearing shorts or trousers you will cycle in and shoes with at most a thin heel. Place the *heel* on the pedal; the leg should be just straight but not stretched at its most extended point (as in the first picture). Next, with the cranks horizontal and the foot in its proper position in the toeclip, the hinge of the forward knee joint should be as nearly as possible vertically above the pedal axle (second picture). Move the saddle backwards or forwards as necessary by loosening the saddle clamp at the top of the seat pillar. Any forward or backward adjustment will also affect the saddle height a little: put it up about 1½mm for every 10mm of forward adjustment, down by the same for backward adjustment. Then check the heel-on-pedal test.

Later you may wish to move the saddle back a bit—up to about 35mm (about 1½in)—but never move it any further forwards. Check that all the clamping bolts are tight, then put a ring of insulating tape round the seat pillar, just touching the top of the seat lug. This will give you an easy check on your starting point if you need to make later adjustments; make them small and stealthy, no more than 2 or 3mm at a time at the most. Any change in position feels odd at first, so give it a week or 50 to 100 miles of use before making any alteration.

You now have to place the handlebar, both horizontally and vertically. An often-quoted method is shown in the third picture: the tips of the fingers are supposed to touch the handlebar bend. This ignores the saddle dimensions and personal variations in arm-to-trunk ratio, so it's not a very good guide. Another method

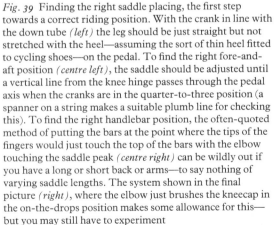

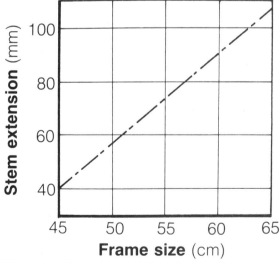

Fig. 39 Finding the right saddle placing, the first step towards a correct riding position. With the crank in line with the down tube (left) the leg should be just straight but not stretched with the heel—assuming the sort of thin heel fitted to cycling shoes—on the pedal. To find the right fore-and-aft position (centre left), the saddle should be adjusted until a vertical line from the knee hinge passes through the pedal axis when the cranks are in the quarter-to-three position (a spanner on a string makes a suitable plumb line for checking this). To find the right handlebar position, the often-quoted method of putting the bars at the point where the tips of the fingers would just touch the top of the bars with the elbow touching the saddle peak (centre right) can be wildly out if you have a long or short back or arms—to say nothing of varying saddle lengths. The system shown in the final picture (right), where the elbow just brushes the kneecap in the on-the-drops position makes some allowance for this—but you may still have to experiment

which allows to some extent for these variables is shown in the fourth picture. The top of the handlebar bend may be positioned according to choice from just below level with the saddle (if you're small) to 40–50mm below.

For average people using frames with the top tube and seat tube lengths about equal there is a rough-and-

Fig. 40 A starting-point correlation between handlebar stem extension length against frame size. Note that this is very much an average figure and individual requirements can differ widely. Extensions longer than these are generally used for racing

ready correlation between stem length and frame size. This is shown on the graph—but remember it is very much an average and wide deviations are possible. Some specialist shops have a fully adjustable mock-up stationary bicycle. Alternatively try just sitting—ignoring pedal position and saddle comfort—on as many different bicycles as possible, and measure the saddle-to-handlebar distance on the most comfortable. In the absence of a measuring set-up this—and trial and error—is the only way, particularly if you have long arms or a long back relative to the rest of your body. The handlebar bends are clamped into the stem so that the lower grip slopes down to the rear a little, say 5 degrees, at the most 10 degrees, to the horizontal.

The position of the brake levers has to be a compromise between having them far enough down for the brake to be easily applied from the drop position and far enough up to rest your hands on. The intrinsic reach of the lever affects this rather. For average-sized hands, having the centre line of the brake lever hood fixing about 35mm (1½in) above the halfway point of the bend is about right; this puts the top of the hood around 15 degrees up from the horizontal.

When complete, your position should be such that when you are stationary, most of your weight should be on the saddle with only the smallest proportion on the bars in the on-the-tops position. Your back should be somewhere between 40 degrees and 50 degrees to the horizontal in the on-the-brake-hoods position and

Fig. 41 You can easily check that both brake levers are at the same height by putting a straight-edge across and comparing it with the top of the handlebar

your upper arm should be somewhere near right angles to your back with your arms straight, rather less with elbows slightly bent as they would be when riding.

Covering the handlebars

There are three common covering materials for the bars: fabric, usually cotton, tape; plastic tapes; and plastic foam padding.

Plastic—usually non-adhesive—is quite long-lasting and readily cleaned but some tapes tend to be slippery in hot or wet weather. Probably the best is the Italian Bike Ribbon which has a thin foam backing, a textured non-slip surface and an adhesive strip. These and other plastic tapes seem to be making a comeback.

Cloth tapes offer a rather surer grip but tend to wear and can become a bit soggy in wet weather. With a very slight degree of padding underneath at salient points they are probably the most comfortable all-round covering. All tape coverings, cloth or plastic, should be wound on beginning from the handlebar end, overlapping about half a turn a time and finishing about 70mm either side of the stem, with the loose end secured by a couple of turns of adhesive plastic tape. In this way the overlaps are not rucked up in use. Cover the section behind the brake hood first with three short (60–70mm) vertical strips of tape to give complete coverage.

Closed-cell plastic foam coatings in tubular form are also available. They have to be pushed on from the end of the bar; obviously the part above the brake lever has to be put on before the lever is fitted. The thinner type is better; the fatter gives a slightly uncertain grip (as well as being rather ugly). To repeat an earlier comment: if you feel that you need heavy bar padding you should first make sure that your riding position is not putting too great a proportion of your weight on your hands and that you are not riding with straight 'locked' elbows.

Finally, the sharp ends of handlebars should be shielded by plastic or rubber end-plugs.

Fitting brakes and gears

Bolt-on brakes are normally fitted in front of the front fork crown and behind the rear seat-stay bridge. The brake shoes into which the brake blocks fit must be the right way round: if they are closed at one end only, that end must face forwards. There should be an arrow or other indication. The shoes should also be adjusted in height until they contact as much as possible of the flat side of the rim: too high and they touch the tyre, too low and only part is in contact. Brakes distort slightly under load and you should check that the leading edge of the shoes does not move up enough to touch the tyre. The shoes should toe in slightly towards the rim.

The cables should follow the shortest path consistent with allowing a smooth curve and leaving ample room for the hands on the bars. Both front and rear should curve to the same height when the front wheel is pointing straight ahead and the rear one should be long enough not to be strained if the bars are inadvertently turned as far as they will go. The length of the outer casing determines this; when cutting outer casing to length, check also that the last strand has not been crimped in. With handlebar extensions of 60mm upwards the natural curve will take the cable behind the bars. The pear-shaped nipple fits into a recess inside the lever. Leave the inner wires uncut until you are sure that you have made all the adjustments necessary and grease them before you put them in. Then cut them so that no more than 10mm or so protrudes beyond the cable clamp on the brake. It can be difficult to re-thread cables once they have been cut. Clean cutting is aided by using the proper tool and by lightly soldering a 20mm length where the cut is to be made.

Gears are more fully documented and the fitting instructions usually explicit. Note that the outer plate of the front gear cage is normally very close to the teeth of the large chainring, perhaps 2mm away.

Most gear assemblies use bare control wire all the way for the front gear and as far as the small stop on the right-hand chainstay for the rear one. The short piece of casing from this stop to the gear should be just long enough to allow the cable to enter the gear mechanism at the correct angle, usually 90 degrees, in all the gear arm positions.

Bottle cages

The best are the simple heavy wire ones, usually aluminium alloy although chromed steel ones are available, Italian Emmepi or French TA, which fit to the brazed on bosses on the down tube by 5mm socket-head bolts. A second bottle can go under the down tube, just in front of the bottom bracket, on the seat tube (which interferes with a frame-fitting pump), or in front of the handlebar stem—which gets in the way of a handlebar bag. If you know you're going to need two, for camping, say, then it's worth getting the second set of bosses brazed on underneath when the frame is ordered. The standard diameter bottle comes in two capacities, 600ml (the usual) or about 900ml.

Fig. 42 A bottle is best carried in a cage like this one bolted to brazed-on frame bosses. The positioning of a second set below the down tube is quite critical: with 26 or 28-tooth smallest chainrings they should be about 60mm and 125mm from the bottom bracket centre

Fig. 44 When using a push-on frame-fitting pump without flexible connector, grip the pump and tyre firmly together to avoid putting sideways stresses on the valve

Fig. 43 The frame-fitting pump nestles between the top and down tubes

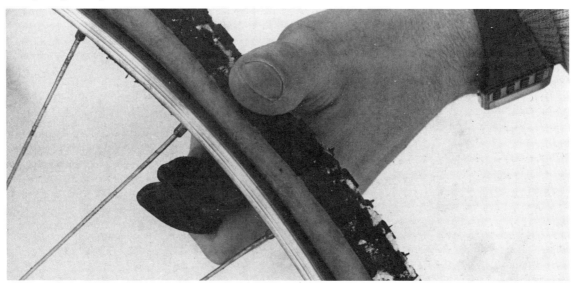

Pumps

The only sort really worth considering for carrying on the bicycle is the frame-fitting type. They come in a range of lengths, each covering about a 35mm frame size range, mostly from West Germany, made by SKS, or from Italy.

Mudguards

Nearly all mudguards are now made from a metal foil/plastic laminate, either in a plain metallic or coloured finish. The same size covers 27in/700 and 26in/650 wheels with smaller ones for 24in/600. Mudguard fittings are one of the bicycle's weak designs with flimsy bits of bent sheet metal to hold them to the brake bolt. The wire stays are held in eye-bolts at the mudguard end and should be cut to length once fitted. Suitable makes are the British Spencer and the West German Esge.

A mudflap should be fitted to the bottom of the front mudguard to keep spray off your feet and the transmission; some are supplied with flaps fitted, some not. The most suitable type has a sort of spade shape about 130mm across and coming down to within about 50mm of the road. You can make a flap from a piece of lorry inner tube rubber or a plastic washing-up liquid bottle or similar container rivetted or bolted inside the mudguard.

FIVE

BICYCLES TO A BUDGET

A custom-built touring bicycle, as a piece of specialised machinery, is not cheap. There are basically three ways of cutting costs: by using cheaper components; by adapting a bicycle; and by buying second hand. All these possibilities demand some mechanical knowledge.

Quite a few bicycles are thrown away because of a written-off frame or wheels, with the durable components such as hubs, handlebar bends and stems, chainsets, brakes and seat pillars eminently reclaimable. If your budget is at rock bottom there is no harm in asking friends, neighbours or relatives if you can tidy out their sheds.

Cheaper components

Very often a cheaper component will be less convenient or more trouble to fit. Cheap steel chainsets have a 'cotter-pin' to hold the cranks to the bottom bracket axle rather than a nice four-sided taper; the saddle clip that holds a saddle to a plain seat pillar comes apart into an amazing number of bits.

Frame Frames can cost from about a quarter that of a custom-built 531 model. There may be seasonal sales, a dealer may be left with a deal that didn't go through, or some may be of intrinsically cheaper but reasonable construction. These bargains will nearly always apply in the 'normal' 21 to 24in (53 to 61cm) range. Measure size and reach carefully, particularly towards the small sizes, and check the size of wheel required as well as clearances and fittings for mudguards.

Wheels About the cheapest aluminium alloy rims are Weinmann Alesa or Wolber Super Champion 58. French Normandy or Atom or Franco/Italian Milremo solid-axle hubs are about a quarter the price of Campagnolo Nuovo Tipo, their quick-release versions about half. 'Rustless' spokes are cheaper than stainless steel. There are often also seasonal sales of wheels. Check that they will fit your frame, both in diameter and rear hub width.

Fig. 45 Normandy solid-centre (i.e. non-quick release) hubs offer reasonable quality at a low price; the rear one is available with fixed sprocket and lockring threading

Brakes I would not suggest any skimping on brakes; the ones suggested in Chapter 3 are near the lower end of the price range for good ones. Avoid cheap steel side-pull brakes.

Chainset There are very few suitable steel cranks on the market and the saving in price is small. There are quite a number of low-price aluminium alloy sets mainly SR and Sugino from Japan and Stronglight from France. The only snag is they are frequently in 170mm only. Check that small chainrings are available.

Gear mechanisms Most manufacturers make cheaper models with a less soigné finish which have the same operating characteristics as their dearer siblings. Examples are the Sun Tour ARX and the Shimano 600 ranges.

Fig. 46 The SR5TG chainset (and the Stronglight 99 and 100, which it closely resembles) is relatively inexpensive and allows rings down to 28 teeth to be used

Saddle This is a personal choice where cost may not be the consideration. Many riders report the cheap Cinelli Unica 55 models to be comfortable and others the Selle Italia 'anatomical' model. Both are about a quarter the price of a top leather saddle. A saddle clip for use with an inexpensive plain seat pillar is cheaper than a pillar with integral cradle but not so easy to adjust to give an exact horizontal mounting.

Pedals The dearest pedals cost about 20 times as much as the cheapest—without considering the really

Fig. 47 The Lyotard range of pedals is inexpensive and includes this double-sided type—a useful feature in traffic

nasty plain-bearing ones. The French Lyotard range is quite extensive and very cheap; pedals and their bearings are in any case very vulnerable and you may prefer to look on them as expendable.

If your budget bicycle has to cope with a limited range of terrain you could consider using only five or six gears with a single chainring. For example a Sugino Maxy chainset, which has a 48-tooth single fixed ring, in combination with a 17–19–21–24–28 Regina freewheel (the only one that will permit a 17T top) you would have a gear range, with 27in or 700c wheels, of 76–68–62–54–46 at almost half the price. Sun Tour and Stronglight BMX models permit interchangeable rings down to 39 and 40 teeth respectively. With a 15–17–19–21–24–28 Maillard Compact 6 freewheel this would give a handy gear spread of approximately 70–62–55–50–44–38.

Adapting a bicycle

There are a number of off-the-peg bicycles now available which approximate to touring requirements: prices range from two-thirds of the price of a custom-built machine to very nearly equal. The market pattern changes rapidly but makers to the fore include Dawes, Peugeot and the Claud Butler badge of the Holdsworthy company. In addition several of the artisan builders such as Mercian, Bob Jackson and F. W. Evans, also supply off-the-peg machines under their own names. The latter make minor equipment specification changes on request, particularly gear ranges and tyres.

The main changes you are likely to need to make to most off-the-peg models concern gears and wheels, plus possibly the saddle.

Almost all bicycles sold have gear ranges that are too restricted and too high for enjoyable touring and you may have to change chainrings, chainset or freewheel. Usually it is not possible to use a front gear mechanism with a largest chain ring size of less than 40 or even 42 teeth because the front chain-shifting 'cage' then fouls the chainstay or gear cable. This precludes the use of small multiple rings with the (probable) existing freewheel of 14 to 24 or 28 teeth. In addition some of the most popular chainsets—the various Campagnolo lookalikes—have a minimum small or intermediate ring size of 42 teeth.

The best solution is to fit a replacement right-hand crank, of the same length, which will accept chainrings of the appropriate 44–36–26 or 46–38–28 size. This also means fitting the appropriate freewheel as in Chapter 3. It *is* possible to retain the commonly fitted 52/42 or 52/40 chainring combination but this will mean changing the freewheel for a Regina 18–21–23–26–31 (the maximum); the gear ranges (78–67–61–54–45 and 63–54–49–44–37) will still be rather high at the bottom end, and the freewheel will be bulky, demanding a long-arm rear gear.

There is currently a tendency to fit narrow rims and tyres to off-the-peg machines and it may be necessary either to have the wheels rebuilt with a wider rim such as the Mavic Module 3 or 4 (of comparable diameter: 700c can well replace 27in) or to buy a completely new pair.

Buying second hand

The usual sources of second-hand bicycles are passed on by word of mouth (often the best), through advertisements in local papers, *Exchange and Mart* or the specialised cycling press (particularly *Cycling Weekly*), or through a dealer. Ideally you should have somebody knowledgeable with you when examining a second-hand bicycle, particularly to check for any accident damage. Some sellers' price expectations are absurd, given the price of new machines; a used bicycle is extremely unlikely to be worth more than about half the new price.

General condition will obviously affect your judgement. Dirt may not detract from efficiency but it is a very good peg for haggling. Certain expendable items have to be replaced on any bicycle from time to time. If these are worn take into account what it will cost to replace them. Roughly in order of speed of wear these are brake blocks, tyres, chain, freewheel sprockets, brake cables, pedals and various bearings (in order; head set, pedals, bottom bracket and hub). Chainwheels, wheels and gear ranges may not be quite what you want so include the cost of replacement in your calculation. Good quality racing wheels may have an appreciable second-hand value if you replace them.

Ask yourself the following questions

Is the frame the right size and shape? *This is fundamental.*

Are mudguard eyes fitted and is there clearance from mudguards (possibly with smaller wheels)?

Do the pedals, with toeclips, clear the front wheel and mudguard in all positions?

Are the frame bearings and other fittings standard and easily replaceable? (French bottom bracket, pedal and freewheel threadings, and Italian bottom brackets and freewheels—when intended for their home markets—are different.)

Are current spares, such as chainrings, available?

Are any components bent? (Check cranks, handlebar bends and stems, pedals, brakes.)

Is there any evidence of crash damage? A frontal collision may push the forks backwards, often on a modern frame by bending the malleable fork crown. Run a straight-edge down the head tube and fork blade. It can also bend the top or down tubes; often you can feel such damage when you can't see it, by running your finger gently along the underside of the two tubes where it may be detected as a very slight ripple. The forks or rear triangle may have been bent sideways—if this is so then the wheels will not be in the same plane. Look along the line of the machine: any gross distortion should be obvious. A more sensitive test is to hold a string or straight-edge across the wheels about 4–5in (10–13cm) above the ground. If the machine is properly 'in track' the straight-edge or cord should be able to be made to touch the wheels at four points, two per wheel. Harsh abrasions on brake levers, handlebars, pedal ends are also thumbs-down indicators.

Finally, insist on riding the bicycle, preferably armed with the diagnostic information in the 'Irritating noises' section of Chapter 12. Riding 'hands-off' in a safe place is another sensitive test of alignment.

A dealer selling a second-hand bicycle will of course be bound by the provisions of the Sale of Goods Act—which says, broadly, that an item must be suitable for the purpose for which it is sold. In a private sale it is up to buyers to satisfy themselves.

SIX

BAGS AND BAGGAGE

What you take with you depends very much on taste and inclination. You could set out with tyre levers, a spare tube, toothbrush and spare pullover—plus a well-filled wallet. You could take food for a fortnight, a tent and a £10 note for emergencies. Or anywhere in between. In remote places—often the most rewarding—you may have to be self-sufficient.

One of the few rigid rules in cycle-touring is that the *bicycle* should do the carrying: except for short distances don't carry anything on your back. A small shoulder bag—a 'bonk bag' in club cyclists' parlance, since it's assumed to carry food—can be very useful to carry personal valuables such as cash, credit cards, passport, tickets and so on, things you might want to keep handy or to remove from the bicycle when you to into a shop or restaurant. It can also be used for carrying food on very short trips, say from the shop to the campsite. Even then it's better strapped onto the top of your regular bags.

A loaded bag anywhere on a bicycle affects the handling, obviously lessened by a light load, keeping it low down and keeping it within the machine's wheelbase. (Unfortunately most of the low-down space within the wheelbase is occupied by whirling feet and legs.) It also helps if carriers are really rigid.

There are basically five positions for bags: as a rear saddlebag, fixed behind and to the saddle; as rear panniers mounted either side of a rear carrier; as a handlebar bag, mounted—preferably—just clear of the centre of the handlebars; as front panniers either side of a front carrier; and as low-mounted front panniers, either side of a carrier near the axis of the front wheel. All have advantages and disadvantages. Most bags are best when full or nearly full; it's better to have a small bag for small loads rather than just drop one or two things into a large but floppy bag.

Traditional bags always used to be made from thick cotton duck, usually black. Like all cotton materials this swelled slightly when damp which made it very water-resistant, while abrasion resistance was excellent. (Cycle bags only wear out where they rub against things, either the carrier or by leaning against walls and

suchlike.) More recently heavy-duty woven nylon in a range of colours, has tended to take over; the later generation fabrics, such as Cordura, are much tougher than earlier rather unsatisfactory materials. Nylon fabric has to be proofed with an impermeable plastic or synthetic rubber layer to make it waterproof. Attention has to be paid to seams, which must be sealed when the weather is wet, since the material round stitching holes doesn't swell. It is desirable in wet weather to line panniers, particularly, with polythene bags. The performance of current lighter gauges of cotton duck and heavier ones of nylon is very similar—and prices not very different. The two major makers of cycle bags in Britain are the two Lancashire cotton-town firms Carradice and Karrimor. Quite a number of small artisan makers have also sprung up. Firms such as Pennine Outdoor and Tor will supply suitable materials for making bags yourself.

For a moderate load (the biggest, the Carradice Camper or the Karrimor Dalesman have a capacity of about 15 litres, plus substantial end-pockets) the traditional saddlebag is fine, providing you are of average build and use a frame in the 21½-24in range. Users of smaller frames may find there isn't room for a saddlebag and larger riders have to take special measures to stop the bag swaying. For small frames Carradice have an ingenious partial solution, their Lowdown model which has a central 'cut-out' straddling the carrier leaving a couple of chubby little legs of bag hanging either side. The usual side pockets are useful for storing things such as tools and maps that you might want on the road. It is best not to carry fragile items in side pockets in case the bicycle falls over. Most saddlebags have loops on top to which a rolled-up waterproof can be strapped. The main advantage of the saddlebag is that it is compact, clear of road mess, fairly easily detached and within the wheelbase. Its main disadvantage is that it carries its

Fig. 48 The five usually used bag positions. *Top to bottom:* conventionally-placed front panniers; rear panniers; low-mounted front panniers; handlebar bag; saddlebag

Fig. 49 Carradice's answer to the low saddle problem: their Lowdown saddlebag has a central cut-out to allow it to fit in the restricted space below the saddle

weight rather high up. Not many saddles nowadays have bag loops but it is possible to fit bolt-on Cyclo ones.

Rear panniers range in size from moderate to gigantic. The large ones are useful for bulky but not too heavy loads such as sleeping bags. There is a temptation, though, to fit very large panniers and then to keep putting things in until they're full. Because rear panniers have to clear your heels, most of their weight lies behind the back axle and they can, if too heavy, make the steering very light or build up a rapid resonant sway at about three cycles per second at speed in extreme cases. You should consider balancing the weight and bulk with front ones.

All rear bags demand a substantial carrier. At the bottom these should be bolted to eyes on the frame rear ends and at the top to the brake bolt, to clips round the seat stays or, best to brazed on eyes or bosses on the seat stays. The most satisfactory carriers are triangulated in three dimensions. Only if a carrier is triangulated in this way (as is the American Jim Blackburn model) will it be truly rigid, irrespective of the number of fixings. Carriers are usually made of steel rod (such as the Tonard or Karrimor models) or aluminium alloy rod (such as the Blackburn). The weak point of aluminium alloy carriers is generally the welding or jointing: check them carefully. Some high-class frame-builders make up carriers from small-diameter steel tube specifically to fit brazed on bosses on their frames—the ultimate, though expensive, solution.

The handlebar bag, the favourite in continental Europe, is now becoming popular in Britain as a 'day-bag' or as a complement to a saddlebag. It shares with the saddlebag the disadvantage of carrying the weight high up but is very convenient to get at and can be protected from the wet by your waterproofs. It is really the only one that you can pop gloves or sunglasses into as you are going along; most have copious little pockets. Most also have a transparent pocket on top to take a map, though you'll struggle to get an Ordnance Survey 1:50 000 in. If the bag is strapped to the handlebar it tends to block the transverse on-the-tops hand position but there are several small carriers available to hold it clear. Do not choose a bag which is so wide that there is no clearance for your hands on the brake hoods. Ideally a handlebar bag should sit as low as possible within the confines of handlebar height and the mudguard. TA and others make a very neat front bag support which fits to the pivot and fixing bolts of a centre-pull brake.

Front panniers are usually about half the size of rear ones (except in France where they tend to carry everything at the front of the bicycle). They can be draped either side of a carrier analogous to a rear one or lower down. In both cases they are a useful longitudinal complement for rear panniers, with the low position (traditional in France, where it originated) much the better for steering stability. Experiment suggests that a weight division of about $\frac{2}{3}$ in rear panniers and $\frac{1}{3}$ in low-mounted front ones offers the best balance and stability. A variety of low-mounting front carriers is available, some with an amazing amount of redundant ironmongery. This is one field where design is evolving quite rapidly, so take a look at the latest available.

As suggested, most bags are best when full or nearly so. Panniers particularly are rather floppy, with corners playing tunes on the spokes when less than full. 2 or 3mm plywood stiffeners the shape and size of the floor of the bags, holding them square, cure this. Rear panniers which tend to shift fore and aft on the carrier can be stabilised by wood block stops on the outside of the bags to engage the carrier uprights.

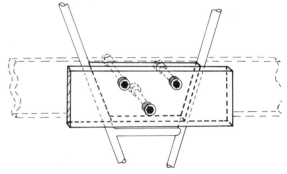

Fig. 50 The prototype—crude but effective—of a simple low-mounting fixing to allow the use of a conventional front carrier. The dotted plywood stiffener on the sketch is inside the bag. It would be advantageous to use plain hardwood with the grain horizontal in place of the outermost piece of ply

SEVEN

LIGHTS AND LIGHTING

During official darkness—from half an hour after local sunset time to half an hour before sunrise—you must use lights if you are riding your bicycle. It can be dark in practice well before official lighting-up time; it's not low light level alone that makes visibility poor but lack of visual contrast too. Lights enable you to see where you are going and other road users to see where you are. As you move from town and traffic to country and solitude, so the balance moves from the latter to the former.

Of recent years a good deal more attention has been applied to devising lighting systems for bicycles, particularly by small inventors who have forced the bigger firms to take notice. There are basically three types of lighting system in use, powered by expendable batteries, by a variety of generators (popularly 'dynamos'), and by rechargeable batteries. There are overlaps.

There is still no fully satisfactory dry-battery lamp available: those with adequate battery life use the D-size cell (approximately 33.5mm diameter and 60mm tall) and have a multiplicity of low-voltage contacts which means that vibration can make them flicker or work intermittently. Those with a neater design and effective contacts, the French Wonderlights, use the low-capacity expensive 4.5v flat battery (approximately 61 by 21mm with rounded corners by 65mm tall). Rechargeable nickel-cadmium ('nicad') cells and batteries to fit are now available for both types; it is necessary to use a charger designed for this type of cell or battery. Makers suggest that the extra life obtained by using alkali-manganese disposable batteries does not offset their higher cost compared with the carbon-zinc type.

Wonderlights and the Ever Ready Nightriders are designed mainly with urban riders in mind and are sold with plastic lamp brackets from which they can be easily detached. Lamps must be fixed to the bicycle and not to the rider and should be mounted on the centre line or offside (see Chapter 13). Take care in mounting any rear lamp to ensure that it cannot be concealed by bags or clothing. In one common position, about half-way down the offside seat stay, lamps are concealed over an appreciable arc by the rear wheel and mudguard. The best position is at the rear of the carrier where they are visible over an angle of 200 degrees or more. Front lamps are best on the front of a front carrier or just ahead of the brake rather than on the front fork, for similar reasons. Clamp-on brackets which can slip down front forks or rear stays are lethal. Rear lamps must (at the time of writing) conform to British Standard 3648; a new standard, part of BS6102, is in preparation and is likely to supersede the earlier one in the appropriate regulations. Lamps which do not conform to the regulations in force may not be sold for use as cycle rear lamps.

There are now two types of tyre-driven dynamo on sale: the conventional bottle-shaped ones and the Sanyo and Byka models, which run on the tread of the tyre and are fitted behind the bottom bracket. The power output is about 3.3w at a nominal 6v, usually divided between about 2.7w (0.45A) for the front lamp and 0.6w (0.1A) for the rear. Some types, particularly the tyre-tread driven ones, tend to deliver markedly higher voltages as speed increases and are desirably fitted with voltage-limiting zener diode devices to avoid blowing the lamp bulbs. Lamp bulbs with higher claimed light output, either with an inert krypton gas filling or using the tungsten-halogen cycle, are available. Tyre-driven dynamos are relatively inexpensive (the tread-driven ones less so), cheap to run, relatively light with a good power output and available for use at any time. Against them is the extra effort needed to drive them, the liability to slip—and hence give no light—in very wet, snowy or icy conditions, and the fact that they go out when you stop. The law allows you to wait unlit by the near side of the road when temporarily halted by road signals or other traffic at night. It is up to you not to stop in stupid or vulnerable positions. Devices which switch on auxiliary batteries when speed drops below a given point are available; one or two of them use rechargeable batteries.

A formerly-marketed alternative type, the Sturmey-Archer Dynohub is built into a lop-sided steel-shelled hub (with 32 or 36-spoke drilling) and has to be built up into its own wheel. It is rather heavier and has a lower output than a tyre-driven dynamo at about 2w, conveniently taken up by a 6v 0.2a (1.2w) lamp at the front and a 6v 0.1a at the rear. If you habitually ride briskly you may need a 0.25a (1.5w) front bulb instead. It is the only lighting system to offer near-absolute reliability irrespective of weather: if the front wheel will go round, the Dynohub will supply power. Unfortunately actual manufacture has recently ceased but it is well worth seeking out remaining stock or secondhand examples.

It is advisable to carry a couple of spare front and rear bulbs for dynamos. Most dynamo sets rely on a return 'earth' connexion via the bicycle frame and have only one wire; if this gives problems the best solution is to insulate lamps from the bicycle and use a double-wiring system.

There are systems available which use small sealed lead-acid (usually 6v) batteries to power mains-rechargeable systems making use of dynamo-type head and rear lamps. If you recharge these lamps regularly they make a very satisfactory lighting system, employing lamps up to 6w in the headlamp, with three to six hours of lighting per charge. Lead-acid batteries are best kept as fully charged as possible at all times.

Generally you have no means of knowing directly whether your rear lamp is lit (and neither has the average car driver his). If you can see it by looking round all well and good, otherwise use every opportunity of checking in shop-window reflections and so on to make sure.

EIGHT

CLOTHING

Clothing depends largely on the weather, so this chapter is divided into warm and mild, cold, and wet sections—with a separate glance at footwear. During fickle seasons such as spring and autumn you might require both warm and cold-weather clothing. Latitude and altitude can also make the summer colder than you expect. All recommendations apply equally to male and female riders. The advice that follows is based on what is practical and comfortable. It's up to you to superimpose your own style.

Warm-weather clothing

When it is warm enough, shorts are the best wear for cycling, the best of these are ones designed for the job. Made of close-fitting stretch material and lined with a special seat, they are designed to be worn next to the skin. The material is either acrylic or nylon-acrylic mixture, which has a matt, slightly woolly texture, or a thinner closer-fitting nylon-Lycra mix, popularly known as 'skin-shorts'. Both types are usually black, although other colours are becoming more common. All cycling shorts and trousers are cut higher than everyday ones at the back of the waist to compensate for the riding position.

The traditional lining for these shorts is chamois leather (or what passes for chamois, since the unfortunate beast is rare enough nowadays to be a protected species). Synthetic linings are much easier to wash and dry, and can even be machine-washed and tumble-dried. This is good news for the cycle-tourist, since chamois leather has to be gently washed with soap and dried slowly if it is not to end up like cardboard. Since these shorts are in effect both outer wear and under-wear they need to be washed as often as underwear would be and it is desirable to have a clean pair daily. We have found it convenient on long trips to have three pairs. In warm climates they dry outdoors in a couple of hours—quicker if they can be spun first. There have been two approaches to these synthetic seat linings, exemplified by the products of the Tyneside firm Been Bag. The first type is a fleecy polyester which looks nothing like chamois and which they have dubbed Polartex. This washes and dries very rapidly but some riders find it a little bulky, too hot in very warm weather (above 25°C, [75°F]), and liable to slight chafing at sustained pedalling rates above 90–95rpm. The alternative cotton-based material with a texture very similar to a soft chamois, Been Bag have named Shamtex. This overcomes the bulk and heat objections but is rather slower-drying after washing. Other manufacturers have broadly similar materials.

If you prefer shorts made of conventional trousering material, check that they are flexible enough for easy pedalling without being liable to ride up between the legs (which causes chafing). Shorts and underwear should be free of seams, particularly transverse ones. All shorts suitable for cycling are rather longer in the leg than you would choose for walking around in.

For the top half of the body the choice is between conventional light shirts or T-shirts—provided they are long enough at the back— and specialised racing-derived cycling tops. These are usually short-sleeved, although you can get long-sleeved versions, long at the back and often with rear pockets, made from polyester, acrylic or acrylic-wool mixtures. Colours are usually bright to lurid, often based on professional sponsored racing teams' colours. It's up to you whether you want to advertise, unpaid, Italian ice-cream firms or French health food shops.

Most riders use cotton or nylon ankle socks in warm weather, while others go sockless or use the 'sockette'-style shoe-liners. It is a matter of bicycling etiquette that ankle socks should be basically white. Avoid very bulky ones.

If you have sensitive hands you may find that the type of mitts used for racing (usually called 'track-mitts') are the answer. These are soft fingerless leather-palmed mittens with a crocheted string back for coolness. They are made in a wide range of sizes and you should choose the tightest-fitting pair you can get on; if you can get them off without rolling them inside-out they're too big. The best are natural light-coloured or chrome leather; darker or coloured versions often have dyes which run.

Cool- and cold-weather clothing

Cycling trousers are either full length with a long zip at the ankle or knee-length and worn with long socks.

The first type—often sold as 'training trousers' or 'training bottoms'—are the cyclist's equivalent of the track suit, and very convenient to slip on over shorts for cool summer evenings or long mountain descents. They are usually made in nylon-cotton or acrylic mixtures, and are generally black. *Any* trousers worn for cycling must be close fitting, particularly round the calf, to ensure that they are well clear of the chain and transmission.

The other type, frequently known as 'plusses', since they are the modern version of plus-fours, are made in a wider range of materials. They can again be of the black stretch cotton-nylon type or from more conventional trousering such as wool-terylene mixes. They have a slight extra fullness at the knee to facilitate pedalling and are then gathered in with an elastic or Velcro fitting below. It is also possible to buy versions with the front and thigh faced with nylon for wet resistance. The most practical combination I have found is to wear terylene-based outer trousers with acrylic Polartex-lined shorts underneath, adding acrylic tights or polypropylene 'thermal' longs—over the shorts, underneath the trousers—when it gets really cold. This principle of layering—having several layers which can be added to or decreased at will—is a recurrent theme in cold-weather cycling clothing. A very thick garment may be very cosy when you're standing still but when you're riding you need to be able to exercise quite fine temperature control. And it is much easier to wash and dry thinner materials. Jeans are not suitable as overtrousers since denim is relatively stiff, they present the perennial seam problem and, worst of all in winter, absorb a lot of water when wet and are poor heat insulators.

In normal cool weather a single pair of adequately long wool socks is enough. They should come well up to the knee to leave no gap at the trouser fixing. When it gets really cold two pairs of socks, a thinner inner pair and a thicker outer, with or without tights, is the answer.

Cycling always seems to be demanding impossible compromises: some form of upper body cover is needed which is completely windproof and insulating while allowing sweat to escape. This is most nearly met by again having several thin layers. Next to the skin it is desirable to have either wool or one of the newer 'thermal' fabrics such as spun polypropylene, as in the Helly-Hansen Lifa range. The layer directly above them should be a porous wool or acrylic material. There are immense personal variations in the degree of sweating and you will have to find out the most comfortable combination. All tops and sweaters must be long enough to cover the lower back.

Proofed nylon cagoules or anoraks are excellent for windproofing and are particularly good for putting on for mountain descents or for hanging about at the tops of hills, but they are sweltering after at the most a few minutes of riding effort. If you like to wear a jacket when cycling then the most practical are of cotton or cotton-nylon, possibly with proofed facing panels on the front, shoulders and arms. The 'breathability' of newly-developed materials such as Gore-Tex is very much on the borderline for the level of moisture raised in active cycling; the published permeability figures suggest that saturation would be reached at quite a modest effort for most cyclists.

When choosing outer garments for use on dark or winter days have regard for visibility. Saturated primary colours or light pastel shades are the most visible in daylight, with yellow and white, either as the whole garment or as panels, showing up more as the light fades. Light and bright socks are also very visible.

Gloves demand the same combination of windproofing and permeability as tops—as you might expect personal tolerances vary enormously. I have found one or two pairs of woollen or acrylic knitted gloves or muffs to be as good as anything, with a homemade pair of fleecy-backed nylon fabric mittens as an additional intermediate layer when it gets really cold. Ski mitts are used satisfactorily by some riders. Avoid impermeable gloves with a fleecy lining which becomes wet with sweat and loses all insulating properties until dried. A pair or two of spare gloves safely dry in the bag can be a near life-saver at times.

In cold weather a hat which covers the forehead can make a tremendous difference to comfort. Woollen hats do this well and are in fact surprisingly waterproof, too. There are also cycling caps sold with a small peak; many riders who wear glasses find the peak helpful.

Wet-weather wear

Dryness and warmth go to some extent hand in hand. The best garment for keeping relatively dry on a bicycle is the old-fashioned all-enveloping cape. A (fairly small) degree of air circulation round the body is retained, certainly more than under an impermeable jacket. It does at least mean that you get less wet from

Fig. 51 One of the popular makes of overshoe for cold or wet days

the inside than you would from the outside without it. It should be big enough to cover you completely with your hands in the on-the-hoods position, giving another 20–30cm (8–12in) of drape over the front of the brake levers, without pulling taut. A properly-sized cape should look utterly ludicrous when you are off the bicycle, leaving a length of leg and ankle showing of which Queen Victoria would have thoroughly approved.

A cape keeps not only the top of the body dry but the arms and the legs to at least the knee as well—with some protection for baggage also. However, this is not to say it has no disadvantages. Riding in a strong wind with a cape can be trying to say the least; oddly enough a head wind isn't too bad, a side wind is awful, with the thing flapping like a schooner in distress and pouring water down your left sock, while a tail wind can tend to lift the cape from behind unless you sit on the last 5–8cm (2 or 3in) of it.

In traffic the inhibiting effect on rear vision and quick signalling is enough for me, at least, to consider it basically unsuitable for town riding. (Hooded cagoules are also bad in traffic for the same reason of restriction of vision—they also deaden hearing.) In the country the cape is the best bet—you'll find you press it into surface as picnic table-cloth, groundsheet, cycle cover and even impromptu bivvy-bag.

Capes are made of translucent textured PVC or, less often, nylon, or a heavier-gauge fibre-reinforced PVC, which is more suitable for winter use. Nearly all capes

sold now are of a highly visible yellow; fluorescent ones, particularly orange, are very trying for anybody riding with you and their visibility fades remarkably rapidly when it gets dark.

Light plastic anoraks or cagoules offer some protection, as do Gore-Tex or similar jackets, but do tend to pick up internal condensation. Because they do not catch the wind so much, they are helpful where a cape is less successful. However, they do leave your legs uncovered.

In general, overtrousers, spats and leggings are more trouble than they're worth, except that you might find that suitable (i.e. not baggy) overtrousers keep non-cycling trousers dry enough over a short journey, say to work.

Feet come in for a fair amount of spray off the road, even with efficient mudguards and mudflaps. The value-for-every-penny school use polythene bags between two pairs of socks (which can make the feet clammy); high-tech devotees use Italian overshoes which cover the foot and 25–30cm of leg, giving the impression of leary blue web-footed strangers from an alien planet.

It is worth taking dry T-shirts or polypropylene vests to put on when you stop. Similarly it's better to carry dry socks than to worry about wet feet.

Fig. 52 Shoes for cycle-touring are made of thin leather, cut low at the ankle and with a shallow heel. They are often also supplied with perforated uppers which can be more comfortable in hot weather

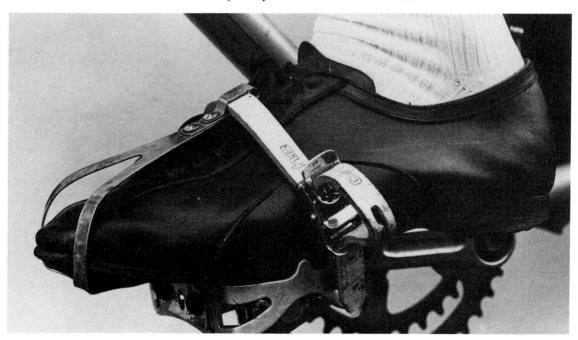

Shoes

Shoes for cycling need to be compact, almost dainty, but with a stiff sole to spread the pedal load. Some racing shoes are virtually impossible to walk in. The uppers of both touring and racing shoes are usually made of thin black calf leather, sewn internally to the sole (what is termed a 'turned' welt); some have perforations in the uppers for ventilation for summer use, while unperforated ones are better for the winter. Most have smooth leather or composition soles and touring shoes a thin heel, perhaps 6mm ($\frac{1}{4}$in). You may find it advantageous for touring shoes to fit rubber stick-on soles before use. Summer shoes should be quite a close fit. For winter you need a pair big enough to take two pairs of thickish socks. Try wearing shoes with the appropriate socks before you buy them. It is also possible to buy nylon fleece-lined shoes or more commonly boots for winter use. Apart from two or three British manufacturers—notably Reynolds of Northampton and Peter Salisbury of Rushden, Northamptonshire (traditional cobbling country) and Arthur Nachman (under the Arturo brand-name) of Leeds—most shoes are Italian. Italian shoes tend to be made on a narrower last than British, and if you have broad feet be especially sure to try before buying.

One further possible addition is shoeplates. These are slotted plates on the sole of the shoe which engage with the rear pedal plate to hold the foot firmly in position. Today many racing shoes come complete with nylon plates, with some position adjustment. They are an aid when you are riding, particularly uphill when you can pull up on a pedal as well as pushing down, provided they are fitted in the right position. They also keep the end of the shoe clear of the toeclip, avoiding pressure on the big toe. Finding the correct position is not too easy: the slot should be about 3–4mm in front of any indentation that the pedal has made on the shoeplateless shoe. Make sure you can extract your foot in an emergency—your straps must not be too tight. Shoeplates are not really designed for novices. Nylon plates are rather quieter but I remember a distinctly embarrassing occasion when our metal-shoeplated party gave an unscored castanet accompaniment to an organ practice in Worcester Cathedral. . .

NINE

CYCLING WITH CHILDREN

Children can enjoy cycling from a very early age—and show it. Most child-carrying has a do-it-yourself element in it; child seats are about the only item obtainable on any scale commercially.

Since many family cycling items are of use to a particular family for no more than a year or two they are often passed on to others. Quite a few, for instance, appear in the small ads of the CTC's magazine *Cycletouring*. The Club's Technical Department suggests that specific 'wanted' advertisements are likely to be more productive than waiting for the right item to be offered for sale. The CTC's Technical Department has, available to members, extremely detailed information sheets including DIY advice on family cycling.

At the age at which they need to spend a large part of the time lying down, and much of that asleep, the only possible way to carry small children is in a sidecar or trailer. These are no longer produced in the numbers they once were although several small firms are willing to consider working on the idea.

We found that the conventional sidecar design, which incorporates a hinge of some form so that the bicycle to which it is fixed can lean over on corners, felt far from positive enough—although it is only fair to add that many others found the Watsonian sidecar of this type quite satisfactory if rather heavy. The expedient we evolved was a rigid frame, fixed to a plate bolted to the bicycle rear fork end with two shallow U-shaped members which dipped to about 15cm from the ground beneath the sidecar body, rising again to support a boss for a full-size side-wheel. A longitudinal member swept forward and up from the two U-pieces to join the down-tube at a clamp just behind the head. This clamp allowed the tracking—the alignment of the sidecar wheel—to be ajusted. Best results were achieved with a very slight degree of toe-in, about 0.5 degrees. It was found necessary to brace the U-pieces by a stay from the seat bolt. The sidecar body was mounted on coil springs on the U-members. The design was intended as an interim one, and a far more elegant development would be possible, but as is the fate of such designs it was used over a period of some

eight or none years, for three children, still in its prototype form.

Although a properly fixed trailer has much less effect on the bicycle's handling than any sidecar does, some parents prefer the thought of having the child alongside and under observation. There are several relatively crude trailers on the market, not specifically designed for child carrying. For this purpose it is essential to have one with proper cycle-type wheels with ball-bearings hubs and pneumatic tyres. Only a few trailers are offered complete with body and you may have to make your own. The few commercial ones have principally fibreglass bodies; if you do not have the skills or facilities for working in this material, I would advise plywood, suitably weatherproofed.

The sidecar or trailer body is essentially a scaled-down pram. In our sidecar the child lay on a foam mattress or sat up against a hammock-style suspended back support. Into the boot behind this support went the indispensable pot and all the sordid paraphernalia of infancy. In all passive child carriers children must be firmly strapped in and protected from getting small hands into any mechanism. It appears that children find the gentle motion of a sidecar or trailer very soothing and ours slept readily. Slightly different lighting regulations apply to sidecars and trailers if you wish to use them in the dark.

Between the ages of about two and five, children can use seats on the back of a bicycle—or tricycle: both Ken Rogers and Pashley make tricycles (or adaptation kits) designed for carrying children. One of the most satisfactory seats ever made was the pre-war Ashby which used a basketwork body—exploiting the natural resilience of wickerwork—with a steel frame. Modern equivalents are plastic mouldings. The seat should have its own mounting, and should incorporate, either in the moulding or separately, some form of guard to keep the child's feet away from the spokes. The rear wheel must also be tough enough to take the load. The centre of balance of the seat has to be fairly well back which can accentuate the whippiness of the bicycle, particularly if it has an open frame. Any other baggage

Fig. 53 This trailer fitment, fixed behind an adult bicycle or even tandem, allows a child to supply some of the effort, but under parental control, without going to the expense of acquiring a special child-back tandem. This model was built by W. Hannington of Reading

is best carried in front panniers, preferably low mounted, to get some form of longitudinal balance. Children need to be firmly strapped in so as they can doze without lolling dangerously. Don't forget that while you are sweating profusely the young passenger will not be working and will need to be effectively clothed against any cold breezes or rain.

At about the age of five the child can take to a real saddle and start some pedalling—on the back of a suitable tandem or a special trailer modelled on the pre-war 'Rann' design. Some tandems are made in 'child-back' form—adult-sized at the front and child-sized at the back. More commonly a subsidiary 'bottom bracket', cranks and pedals are fitted part-way up the rear seat tube of a conventional tandem. The device generally drives to the left side of the rear bottom bracket, but the neatest arrangement I have seen drives direct to the front bottom bracket of the tandem. This is used for the main drive, allowing a fair range of height adjustment without having to alter chain length. Special juvenile cranks (steel with cotter-pin fitting) may be used or crank shorteners are available to bring adult cranks down to child length with the penalty of making them splay their legs more.

The expense of rigging up a tandem can be quite considerable and an alternative is the Rann-type trailer. This is a child-sized half-bicycle which is fixed by a hinged mounting to the rear of a bicycle (or, rather more cumbersomely, adult tandem). The vertical-axis rotating joint takes the place of the conventional head tube, front fork and front wheel.

The amount of work that a child does on a Rann trailer or on the back of a tandem varies; they go through phases of pushing their own weight or apparently not trying at all. Once again, although the child contributes some effort, it will not be working at anything like the rate of the adult and accordingly will need more clothes in cool conditions.

From the age of six or seven a child can learn to ride a proper bicycle. Frames can be made down to about 16in (40cm) to take 600A (32–540, 24 × 1¼in) wheels for which quite good quality components are available. A lightweight frame to this size will be no cheaper than a larger one—possibly dearer since it will require an individual design—so you will have to weigh up its potential usefulness. We had a 47cm (18½in) frame made up because there were three users lined up. Such a frame will have a second-hand value; ours has served several others since. A bicycle built in this way should be designed to use short cranks and have a correspondingly low bottom bracket height. The sizings given in Chapter 2 are still generally applicable, based on inside leg measurement.

Cycling with children

While children are small enough to spend quite a lot of time asleep, they can do it as readily in a sidecar or trailer as anywhere else. However, as they progress to seats, tandems and so on you will have to accept that the *hours* spent actually cycling will have to be curtailed. A child is likely to have a far shorter endurance before becoming tired, or bored, than an adult. Your trips will need to be punctuated by stops to look at interesting things or to play or paddle.

TEN

CYCLING WITH DISABILITIES

In August 1983, Bernard Migaud of Metz in France stood on his one leg and his faithful metal *pilon* at the top of the Col de l'Iseran, 2770 metres above sea level and the highest 'natural' road col in Europe. He had already qualified for membership of the 'Club des 100 cols' by cycling up a hundred mountain climbs, of which—to qualify—five had to rise to over 2000 metres. On 24 August 1985, Hugh Culverhouse of Penn in Buckinghamshire reached John o' Groats at the north-east corner of Scotland 3 days 5 hours 56 minutes and 17 seconds after leaving Land's End in Cornwall, 1360km away. Following an irreparable fracture of the femur at the age of 18, Culverhouse had, for fifteen years, the use of only his right leg for propulsion.

Both these riders, and others who have ignored comparable handicap, are obviously people of extraordinary determination—as this book was being written, Hugh Culverhouse was making plans to ride across America—but their exploits demonstrate that cycling is possible even with extreme disability. Other riders have ridden happily—sometimes unremarked—with one prosthetic limb.

The value of graded exercise in rehabilitation is nowadays fully recognised, and the bicycle, because of its smooth rotary leg motion, has assisted many people to recover physical faculties after injury or stroke. Initially such exercise should be part of a progressive medically supervised programme, but there are nevertheless documented cases of determined riders defying unfavourable prognoses.

Very low gears are needed: in many cases it will be much easier to remain mounted once installed (certainly Bernard Migaud's experience) and in any case speeds and power available will be lower. TA and Stronglight chainrings down to 26 and 28 teeth respectively, and Sun Tour freewheels with 30, 32 or 34 tooth sprockets permit gearing down to 20in

Getting on the bicycle may pose some problems and it is possible that an open frame, perhaps one of 'mixte' design, may be of advantage. A tricycle is a possibility since it permits the rider to stop, if forced to by traffic or simply for a rest on a hill, without having to get off. It must be pointed out, though, that tricycle riding demands the mastery of a new riding technique, since the machine cannot be leaned for cornering.

Stiffness, the results of injury or arthritic conditions, of knees, hips or ankles of either or both legs may restrict joint movement. Small degrees may be accommodated by using short cranks; if the condition is a long-term one it could be worth considering a specially made frame with a low bottom bracket. TA 5-pin cranks go down to 150mm; other shorter ones, in steel with cotter-pin fitting and fixed rings, are made for children's bicycles. Alternatively, as noted in Chapter 9, it is possible to obtain crank shorteners, although the increase of 45–55mm in width of tread may be unacceptable here. The reduced leverage of short cranks will increase knee loading for a given effort, so lower gears are necessary.

If only one leg is affected it is possible to fit a specially designed shortened and swinging crank to that side, which allows the foot of the stiff leg to follow a lower and smaller diameter circle. Such devices, individually made to compensate for each rider's personal movement limitations, are offered by Ronald Rice of Bedford. In this way the affected leg can supply a smaller but still useful part of the work of pedalling.

Unequal leg length is relatively common and may pass unnoticed while cycling. The general rule is that if there is no discomfort then no alteration should be made to the bicycle. If necessary, it is possible to pack up pedal plates to compensate: this is generally more satisfactory for cycling than the use of a built-up shoe. TA supply rather expensive pedals with unequal side-plate heights: alternatively it is quite easy to make bolt-on extensions from aluminium strip or sheet of the appropriate thickness, about 1.5 to 2mm. The consensus view is that the plates of the pedal for the shorter leg should be higher by about $\frac{2}{3}$ of the difference in leg length.

There have also been successful riders with only one arm; the national 25 and 30-mile tricycle records were at one time held by a one-armed rider. It is possible to obtain double-cable brake levers (e.g. Dia-Compe 144T) which apply two brakes with one lever (although it is doubtful whether this would make the two braking systems 'independent' as required by law). Adaptations have also been made permitting a rear brake to be operated by the left heel. Other adaptations have been stops, supports and fixings to accommodate a prosthetic arm, and built-up supports for arms shorter than the other.

Blind riders have been enabled to enjoy the feel and open-air freedom of cycle-touring by riding on tandems with sighted partners. There are long-standing contacts between some cycling clubs and CTC local groups, and blind schools. There is a registered charity, 'Tandems for the Blind', to promote such contacts and to provide suitable machines.

People with an impaired sense of balance have also successfully ridden on tandems and on tricycles. Three firms, Ken Rogers, George Longstaff and George Fitt Engineering, have built tricycles and tandem tricycles for the partially handicapped.

One of the services offered to members by the CTC is information on cycling with disabilities. Many of the small but ingenious adaptations have been developed by disabled riders and their engineer friends to overcome particular disabilities; as far as possible the CTC's Technical Department acts as a clearing house for such ideas.

ELEVEN

ESSENTIAL MAINTENANCE

This chapter deals with routine maintenance of the bicycle, the sort of attention necessary to keep it running smoothly. There are many topics beyond the scope of an introductory textbook such as this so you will *not* find sections on, for example, wheelbuilding or reassembling a gear from its component pieces. There are more detailed, and more expensive, books on the subject: the generally accepted definitive work is Howard Sutherland's *Handbook for Bicycle Mechanics*, and details of this and others appear in Appendix 2. Some items of bicycle equipment come with quite specific fitting and servicing instructions; most do not.

The elements of maintenance fall into five main divisions: cleaning; lubrication; general and specialised tools; adjustment; and full servicing with possible replacement. Obviously these overlap to some extent; it would be stupid to replace, say, front hub bearings without cleaning, lubricating and adjusting them. Finally, since there's little point in maintaining the mechanical condition of your machine unless you also maintain ownership, the chapter concludes with a note on parking and locking.

Cleaning

Road dirt accumulates under mudguards and on frame tubes and is best washed off with warm water, either soapy or lightly dosed with detergent. Road salt, from treated winter roads, or marine salt, if you're touring near the sea, should be washed off, even with plain water, as soon as possible.

Wheels inevitably acquire a grey slime of rubber and abraded alloy from using the brakes in the wet. Lightly scrub rim and tyre with a dash of a fine household abrasive cream cleaner such as Jif or Ajax, using Brillo pads if needed to remove rubber from the rims. This also cures brake squealing caused by oil or grease on the rim.

Brakes too should be cleaned of road dirt and the blocks themselves cleaned of any embedded grit or metal particles.

Most greasy parts such as chainrings, cranks gears and hubs merely need wiping with rag or paper towel. Heavy dirt can be removed by brushing with a paraffin- or diesel-soaked brush, such as an old toothbrush, followed by wiping clean. The most effective way of cleaning between the sprockets of a multiple freewheel is to remove heavy deposits with an old spoke, completing the cleaning by scrubbing to and fro with a piece of paraffin-soaked stout string.

The chain should be cleaned by physically brushing or scraping off as much as possible of the inevitable greasy mud/oil compound, then brushing it with the paraffin-soaked brush and wiping clean. Removing the chain and soaking in petrol or paraffin is not a good idea, particularly with chains such as Renolds which have a proper inner roller bush and outer roller construction: this is because it is not too easy to replace effectively the manufacturer's internal lubricant.

If you want to shine up a frame either a car polish or a wax furniture polish will brighten it and the mudguards, and to some extent act as a water-repellent. If aluminium alloy parts are satin-anodised, a soft silver-grey sheen, all that metal polish will do is to damage the anodic film.

Lubrication

The major bearings of the bicycle—head, hubs, bottom bracket and pedals—are nowadays designed to be fully serviced relatively infrequently rather than lubricated at shorter intervals. Good quality bearings have such close clearance between axle or cone and shell that when properly greased they are, for practical purposes, sealed. Industrial 'sealed' ball or roller bearings are not entirely satisfactory on bicycles, partly because industrial sealing was never intended to stand up to salt-spray and road dirt, partly because the traditional cup-and-cone bearings are self-aligning under the distortions produced by pedalling and loading to a degree which is often not appreciated. A new generation of sealed units, designed for bicycle applications, is emerging.

Head bearings, kept properly adjusted, will run almost indefinitely unless left upside down in the wet, as on some car roof-racks. (With an upside-down rack smear a thin 'seal' of grease round the entries to the top and bottom head races before travelling.) **Hub and bracket bearing** may require stripping down perhaps once a year, pedals possibly more often: see the 'adjustment' section below. For all these bearings a soft, preferably waterproof, grease such as Castrol LM, CL or Medium is suitable; harder greases leave the bearings running in channels which can fill with water.

A light oil is the best lubricant (applied from a fine-spouted can, not by aerosol) for brake pivots, the points where brake springs bear against stops, hub quick-release lever bearings, front and rear gear parallelogram pivots and toe-strap pivots.

Freewheels need a light oil, too; however, since freewheel bearings vie with the inboard end of the pedal for the title of the bicycle's most vulnerable bearing, it may be preferable to service the freewheel fully at intervals. It is not easy to lubricate a freewheel properly when it is mounted on a hub, although you may have to. Lay the wheel down as near horizontally as possible, freewheel downwards, wipe the back of the freewheel clean as far as possible and run a line of oil round the entry to the rear bearing, turning the freewheel and repeating until clean oil comes out the other end. Wipe off all excess, repeating the wiping as needed over the next day or so. The first place that oil dripping out of a freewheel goes to is via the spokes onto the rim and tyre. Lean a bicycle with a recently-oiled freewheel so that any drips fall clear.

The **chain** has more bearings than the rest of the bicycle put together, all of them out in the weather. New high-tech lubricants seem to work in dry conditions, when an oil might pick up road dust to make an abrasive mixture. In the wet and even more in mud, snow or slush, oils or oil-based chain lubricants such as Castrol's are more effective, though you have to remove the incredibly sticky black deposit that builds up. Since chain bearing action is a sliding one, oils containing compounds with slippery layered crystal structures—such as graphite or molybdenum disulphide—also work well. One American authority has recently concluded that paraffin-wax (candle-wax), applied by immersing the cleaned chain in a molten pot of the substance, is better than anything else.

Cables are best greased during assembly with a smear on the inner wire and a small blob in the end of the casing so that the wire pushes it through. Straddle-wire channels on brakes and bottom bracket tunnels for gear cables should also be kept greased. Fancy plastic-coated brake wires (e.g. Aztec) are designed to be assembled and left dry.

Tools

Tools for bicycle maintenance divide into two categories, general tools and those specific to bicycle components, or even specific makes. Some are really essential, others are useful to acquire as the need arises. Some you need to carry with you, some are workshop items.

General tools

Spanners Despite the range of dumb-bell or multiple spanners sold by cycle shops, the best are proper staightforward engineering open-ended spanners, plus possibly one or two ring, socket or tubular spanners. It is difficult to set adjustable spanners accurately enough for small sizes but they are quite acceptable from 15mm upwards. Nearly all bicycle nuts are metric nowadays (except bolts on steel cotter-pinned chainsets ($\frac{3}{16}$ in Whit), and front and rear track nuts ($\frac{1}{4}$ and $\frac{5}{16}$ in Whit respectively) for which a 120mm long $\frac{1}{4} \times \frac{5}{16}$ Whit double-ended ring spanner is the best bet). For everything else, except possibly TA chainring bolts, open-ended spanners are more versatile. 8×9mm, 10×11mm, 12×13 and 14×15mm—possibly 16×17mm—should cover most requirements, although there isn't a lot of call for 11, 13 or 14mm. The following tabulation shows where most are used:

8mm TA chainring bolts; mudguard stay fixings (outboard end); lamp fittings; gear mechanism cable clamps; gear front mechanism frame clamps, rear gear chain tension roller bolts; gear lever frame clamps.

9mm brake shoe adjustments; most brake cable clamps, including centre-pull straddle-wire hangers, some brake lever fixing bolts (these really need a tubular spanner); a few gear cable clamps; toe-clip bolts.

10mm most brake fixing bolts; some brake shoe adjustments; all nuts on Weinmann centre-pull brakes (except cable clamps).

12mm Mafac centre-pull brake arm pivots.

13mm or 14mm some seat pillar saddle-cradle clamp bolts.

Fig. 54 It is best to buy good quality metric spanners and allen keys from a specialist engineering tool shop

15mm pedal spindle flats (for removing or fitting pedals).

16mm or 17mm some hub lock nuts; some crank extractors.

One or two rare oddments such as brake cable clips for frames without guides and very few gear mechanisms require smaller, 7 or even 6mm, spanners.

Allen keys Modern fittings are making increasing use of neat socket-head fittings. The usual sizes are 4, 5 and 6mm:

4mm some mudguard stay (fork-end) bolts; bottle cage bolts; front gear mechanism frame clamp bolts; gear lever frame clamp bolts; brake-lever clamp bolts; a few gear mechanism fittings or adjustments; TA chainring bolts.

5mm frame seat lug seat pillar clamps; a few rear gear chain tension roller bolts; Sanyo and similar tyre-tread dynamo clamps; most chainring bolts apart from TA; rear gear fixing bolts.

6mm handlebar stem expander bolts; handlebar stem handlebar bend clamp bolts; auxiliary fitting on some pedal spindles and pedal caps; some seat-pillar saddle cradle bolts, a few bottom bracket axle end-bolts; some rear gear fixing and tensioning bolts; some rear gear cable clamp bolts.

Some older, particularly Italian, handlebar stems have 7mm expander bolt fittings. Some recent chainsets have a 6 or 7mm captive-bolt fitting for fastening and removal.

Using spanners and allen keys Many bicycle components make use of aluminium alloys and it is vitally necessary to acquire a feel for the intrinsic strength of these and other materials to avoid stripping threads or breaking such items as clamps. Most bolts are tightened up until some member is clamped tightly enough for it not to move under normal usage. You must learn to sense the torque necessary to achieve this, and when to stop. It is impossible to describe, but quite easy to feel, when you stop tightening and begin to plastically deform metal. Don't extend spanners or keys with pieces of tube to undo a refractory component.

The smaller hexagonal-headed nuts or bolts, the 8mm TA chainring ones particularly, demand care in fitting the spanner to the flats of the hexagon. A small socket or ring spanner such as a Zeus or Campagnolo combined 6mm allen key and 8mm socket spanner helps.

Screwdrivers Slotted-head bolts are fast disappearing from cycle equipment. Some mudguard fittings and lamps still require them, as do frame fork-end adjusters, toeclip bolts and spoke nipple heads. A stubby one with a 5mm blade and a small electrical one are the most useful. Phillips-head bolts are used mainly for gear stop adjustment and also in some lamps. A cross-head screwdriver with a 2.5 or 3mm blade is suitable.

Special tools

Cone spanners These are thin spanners, usually 13, 14 and 15mm, which engage the narrow flats on hub cones.

Peg and C-spanners Peg spanners tighten some headsets and left-hand bottom-bracket cups, while C-spanners tighten their lock-rings, as well as lockrings for fixed-gear sprockets.

Freewheel removers These are hardened steel cylinders with pegs or splines to fit slots or meshing splines on the freewheel body at one end, and with external flats at the other. The flats are best gripped with a vice or large adjustable spanner. Different makes of freewheel require different removers; Sun Tour and Maillard Compact, however, have a similar fitting.

Chain bearing pin extractor This invaluable device is a small vice which holds the chain while a small punch, advanced by a fine-thread screw, pushes the bearing pin (or 'rivet') through the sideplate to break or reassemble the chain. The same model suffices for all chains except the $\frac{1}{2} \times \frac{1}{8}$ in Renold Elite model which has shouldered pins which will not pass through the sideplates.

Crank tools These are virtually essential for removing cranks and helpful for fitting them. They are specific to each make or even model, although there are some overlaps. The extractor part comprises a threaded outer which screws into the thread on the crank, and a snub-nosed centre part, threaded to fit into the outer. By screwing this inner part inwards, the snub end bears on the end of the axle and pushes the crank off the axle taper. The reverse end, or a second separate part, is a socket spanner for the axle end bolt.

Spoke nipple key A small specialised spanner which fits the squared portion of a spoke nipple for adjusting spoke tension. 14 or 15swg spoke nipples have the same size square; 12 or 13swg are larger and require a separate key. Bent metal spoke keys are almost useless.

Fig. 55 Three special bicycle tools which make the impossible possible: *top to bottom*—chain bearing pin ('rivet') extractor (and replacer); crank fitting and removing tool (this is an SR version); freewheel remover—this one fits Sun Tour and Maillard freewheels

Fig. 56 Three workshop tools for specific job. *Top to bottom:* secateur-style brake and gear wire cutters; peg spanner with replaceable pegs; thin spanners for hub cones

Sprocket remover A vicious-looking piece of mugging equipment comprising a steel bar 25–30cm long with a length of bicycle chain attached which removes a single fixed sprocket from a hub or tightens up a sprocket or freewheel. Two together may be used to remove sprockets from a freewheel body.

Cable cutters It *is* possible to cut brake and gear inner wires with care using side-cutting pliers but one snip with the proper tool leaves a square end which can be rethreaded.

Other specific tools Some headsets require non-hexagonal spanners to adjust them properly, and some pedal caps are extraordinarily hard to get off or replace firmly without the pastry-cutter-shaped ring spanner that fits them. Some crank and bottom-bracket-fitting makers supply special ring versions of the C-spanner which engage several lockring notches at once, giving a firmer grip.

Adjustment

This section considers adjustment alone; the following section covers full stripping down and possible replacement.

Bearings

All bicycle bearings involve a cup-and-cone type of bearing, although the movable part may be the inner cone or outer cup according to which bearing it is. A properly adjusted bearing should revolve freely without any detectable unevenness or grating but should at the same time be free of any play or shake. A *very* small degree of play is to be preferred to over-tightening. Play is much more apparent if wheels are checked at the rim and bottom brackets at the pedal end of the crank.

All the bearings except the freewheel have some form of locking ring or nut. Bicycle threads are rather imprecise, so the final tightening up of the locking device will alter the beautiful precision of your adjustment. Because the locknut bears inwards on the bearing, headsets, hubs and pedals will tend to become *tighter* when you do up the locknut; because the lockring of the bottom bracket bears against the bottom bracket shell, tending to push the cup outwards, this bearing tends to exhibit *more* play when the locking ring is tightened. Allowing for such perverse behaviour is part of the black art of bearing adjustment. Depending on the matching of the threading this compensation amounts to some 5–30 degrees of rotation of the bearing cone or cup.

Hubs In hubs the balls run in cups inserted in the hub flanges and run on the curved surfaces of the cones which are threaded onto the axle. The axle has a small slot cut into it and next to the cone comes a flat tongued washer whose function is to prevent turning the locknut turning the cone as well. Using the thin cone spanners (usually 13mm for a front hub, 14 or 15mm for a rear) to hold the cone still, undo the locknut with the appropriate spanner. With the cone spanner, tighten the cone gently until the bearing feels correctly adjusted. Then turn the cone *back* through about 15 degrees to allow for the locknut effect and begin to tighten the locknut slowly, checking the bearing for freedom of movement. If signs of overtightening show, reverse and step the cone back another few degrees; if the bearing still shows some shake, then reverse and repeat with the cone tightened again by a few degrees. Overtightening any bearing can form indentations in the cones or cups.

Pedals After removing the pedal cap the procedure is very similar to that for the hub, but less accessible. Hold the pedal spindle firm by means of a 15mm spanner on the flat next to the crank.

Headset The difficulty here is usually that of holding the top race (which is one cup of the bearing) firmly while you tighten the top nut down if it has no proper flats or other holding device. If it has flats they may need a special spanner like a big cone spanner. Top nuts and the 'fixed' cups of bottom brackets are large enough for an adjustable spanner.

Bottom bracket The odd one out. First of all, if the bearing does show play, check that the *left-hand-threaded* 'fixed' cup on the right-hand side has not become loosened. If it has, remove the right-hand crank and tighten the cup firmly home before you tackle the other side. It will usually be simpler to remove the left-hand crank to adjust the movable cup. Undo the lockring and adjust the cup: most require a peg spanner. Then begin to tighten the lockring gently. If play develops, tighten the cup gently to take up the shake without altering the lockring position and then begin to tighten the lockring further. Repeat in small steps until the lockring is tight and the bearing correctly adjusted.

Freewheel If a freewheel develops play (for on-the-road symptoms, see Chapter 12) the only way of taking it up, on all except Sun Tour New Winner models which have an adjustable cone, is by undoing the freewheel lockring (which has a *left-hand* thread) by means of a drift or soft punch, removing one of the thin metal shims inside, and retightening. This is most easily done with the freewheel left firmly on the wheel

hub, so that the solid centre of the freewheel is tightly held. If you want to carry out any of the work in the next section, loosen this lockring by half a turn *before* you take the freewheel off the hub. Do not remove it completely or the freewheel remover may damage the lockring threading.

Brakes

Brakes may require two routine adjustments, to adjust the position of the blocks and to compensate for brake block wear.

As blocks wear and shape themselves to the rim the top part can touch the tyre. If the block has worn so that a thin lip of rubber at the bottom follows the curve of the rim section, trim the surface of the block level, with a craft knife or stout scissors. The nuts holding the brake shoes can then be loosened and the block moved up or down, and its alignment with the rim changed, as necessary. Make, or at least check, all changes with the blocks pulled in to touch the rim. As the brake is applied, blocks move up or down relative to their rest position. Centre-pulls such as the Mafac Racer move up as they are applied; brazed-on cantilevers and side-pulls move down.

Wear on the blocks may be taken up in two ways. The screw adjusters, at the brake hood (e.g. Mafac) or at the brake or hanger (e.g. Weinmann), may have enough threading to bring the blocks back to their proper position relative to the rim, with a 2–3mm clearance when off. If not screw the adjusters back to their lowest position and pull the inner wire through. This involves loosening the cable clamp bolt, holding the brake blocks against the rim with one hand and pulling the cable through with the other. If the clamp bolt is not completely undone there will be enough friction to hold the wire in place while you do the clamp bolt up again. When released the tension of the brake spring should be enough to pull the blocks back to the right clearance. Any small deficit can be taken up by the screw adjusters.

Gears

The throw of the gears should be checked: they should not derail the chain off the bottom and top sprockets or rings but should nevertheless change into the extreme positions positively. The screw stops limiting the movement may have to be altered to achieve this. The inner wires of the cable should be just slack with the levers fully forward with ample movement to cover all the gears. Any slack is taken up by pulling the wire through the cable clamp.

Fig. 57 The two adjusters (marked 'L' for low and 'H' for high) limit the throw of the rear gear towards bottom and top respectively. They bear against the arrowed surfaces at the end of the gear's travel

Full servicing and replacement

This section covers stripping down, checking and, if necessary, replacing worn bearings, brake blocks and cables. Other items wear out in time but are merely removed and replaced by new ones; such items are tyres, pedals, chain, freewheel sprockets and chainrings.

A word of caution on the transmission: chains wear

Fig. 58 Cones showing typical bearing surface wear. *Top,* unused cone with fine ground surface; *centre,* used cone with bearing track polished smooth by the balls—perfect for further use; *bottom,* cone with pitted bearing track—ripe for replacement

on the bearing pins and rollers, the 'pitch'—the distance from link to link—becomes slowly greater, and freewheel sprockets, or the most-used ones, become worn to match. A new chain with its precise pitch does not mesh perfectly with the used freewheel sprockets and tends to jump under load. It is usually best therefore to replace chain and freewheel sprockets at the same time. Since chains wear out rather faster than freewheels, it is possible to fit a new chain after, say, 2000km, keeping the old one. After a further 1500–2000km replace the original chain for another spell, and so on, alternating the chains, so that both chains and the one set of sprockets wear out in stages together. Three chains and shorter intervals would be even better.

Bearings

Wear in bearings manifests itself as noises when riding, and difficulty in adjusting satisfactorily. With hub, bottom bracket and pedal bearings the inner cone part of the bearing or axle wears many times faster than the cups. In head bearings the wear is more evenly divided but even so the inner surfaces, particularly the fork crown race, wear faster. One would expect to have to renew a head set complete.

Once you have taken the bearing apart you should check the vulnerable parts for wear. On a used but still healthy cone or axle surface the track along which the balls run is visible as a shiny line; on worn bearings this shiny track is broken up and pitted over part of its circumference. It is best to replace the item if the wear is at all marked.

Hubs To dismantle, undo the locknut at one end and unscrew it and the cone completely. Lay the wheel down on a sheet of paper or plastic and lift out the axle from the other end. The balls should either fall out or be easily persuaded out. Wipe everything completely clean with a paper towel or rag. If there is any rusting, discolouration or surface pitting of the balls throw them away and replace. Examine the cones for wear and replace if necessary; if you do not know the exact type of hub you are using, then take the old cones along when you go to buy a replacement so that they can be matched. Put a thickish smear of new grease in the hub cups and place the balls in one by one. Most front hubs take $9\frac{3}{16}$in (5mm) ones and the rear $9\frac{1}{4}$in (6.5mm). If the balls are in cages, replace in position, with the more closed side of the cage towards the cone. Put more grease in after you have inserted the balls, replace the spindle and then screw the other cone back into place, following it by the locking washer, any spacers and the locknut. Readjust and wipe away surplus grease.

Pedals As for hubs, except that the crank-end cone is an integral part of the axle. This inner bearing, although vulnerable to the weather, will stand a lot of abuse and there is no point in panicking to replace a slightly pitted axle provided the pedal will run quietly and reasonably smooth. Pedals take varying numbers of $\frac{1}{8}$ or $\frac{5}{32}$in balls.

Bottom bracket Remove both cranks and then undo the lockring and left-hand adjustable cup completely. Carefully withdraw the axle, catching any balls that come out with it. You will probably have to fish inside for most of them. Wipe axle, cups and balls clean with paper towel and inspect for wear. If necessary, replace. The load on the right-hand bearing of a bottom bracket axle is almost all during the part of the pedal stroke when the right-hand crank is between one and four o'clock, and the load on the left-hand opposite this. It is possible to prolong the life of a partly-worn axle by refitting the cranks 90 or 180 degrees away from the original position. You could rotate them 90 degrees on a routine basis, around every 2000–3000km, as a preventive measure. Grease and replace the balls; bottom brackets take either 11 loose $\frac{1}{4}$in balls or a smaller number in a cage. Once again the more closed end of the cage goes towards the cone bearing of the axle. Replace the adjustable cup in position and readjust. Wipe off surplus grease: remember that the taper flats on the axle and the inside of the crank which fits on them must be clean and dry when you put the cranks back on.

Headset The three bottom components of the headset, the crown race and the two frame races, are tight push fits onto the fork crown and into the head tube. Only replace these items yourself if you are confident that you can tap the replacements into position accurately, completely and squarely; if not get it done professionally. Otherwise remove the handlebar stem, and possibly the front brake. The remaining stages are best carried out with the bicycle upside down to keep the cascade of tumbling balls in check. In this position the cup part of both races is downwards. Unscrew the top locking nut and the top adjustable bearing completely and remove the balls carefully, while keeping the two halves of the fork crown held together. Then lift the fork gently free, removing any balls which adhere to the bearing on the fork crown. This bearing particularly should be checked for pitting. On head bearings this shows up as regular round indentations in the ball track. The main load on the head bearing is compression or impact from the road shocks with relatively little rotational wear. Clean all bearing surfaces and the balls, regrease and reassemble. Different makes of headset use $\frac{1}{8}$in, $\frac{5}{32}$in or $\frac{3}{16}$in balls, and

Fig. 59 How a freewheel works. When you're pedalling, the ratchet teeth of the outer part which is driven by the sprocket engage the spring-loaded pawls *(arrowed)* and turn the inner part which is screwed onto the hub. When you're freewheeling the inner part is moving while the outer isn't and the pawls click over the shallow slopes of the ratchet. If the pawl springs are broken or gummed up the pawls don't engage so the freewheel freewheels both ways

some, rollers. Most lightweight ones are nowadays supplied with caged races.

Freewheel The freewheel will repay taking apart and cleaning rather more frequently than the other bearings since it is very vulnerable to the ingress of water and road dirt. Loosen the lockring as described in the 'Adjustment' section above, and then remove the freewheel from the hub. Use the quick-release or a track nut as appropriate to hold the pegs ('dogs') of the freewheel remover into the slots on the freewheel. You will have to undo this fixing in step with unscrewing the freewheel. Complete the removal of the loosened lockring and then lift out the thin pieces of metal shim beneath it. Carefully invert the freewheel, collecting the balls on paper or plastic. Then lift the centre boss of the freewheel out from the back to expose the back row of balls. There may well be a muffled 'ping' at this stage as the pawls spring free from the ratchet. On Regina freewheels the pawls are near the rear of the

freewheel and are quite unrestrained. On Maillard ones the pawls and ratchet are at the front and are partially held back from flying out; on Sun Tour freewheels they are again at the front but cleverly held so that the inside taper of the sprocket-bearing part eases them back into place when you reassemble it. You have to take different measures (as illustrated) with the others. Check that both pawl springs are present and working—otherwise replace. The most satisfactory way to remove all dirt and contaminated lubricant is to immerse the parts of the freewheel in paraffin or petrol (well out-of-doors); an ideal container is a moderate-sized aluminium foil pie tray. Allow solvent to dry off the freewheel, wipe clean and then examine the ball tracks. If they are pitted or lightly corroded a rub round with fine emery cloth to smooth them is well worth while. As with pedals, a little pitting is no cause for panic. Wiped clean, lightly smear the ball tracks with grease and replace the balls on the back (larger) bearing. Freewheels use $\frac{1}{8}$in balls in inordinate numbers (somewhere above 70). Check that the pawl springs are functioning and restrain the pawls as shown in the illustrations. Carefully lower the central part into the sprocket-bearing outer which should be lying top-sprocket downwards. Replace the balls in the front bearing and any shims and tighten up the *left-hand-threaded* lockring. It must be really tightly done up. Then run a little light oil into the freewheel from the back. It should run smoothly and quietly apart from a self-satisfied oily click.

It is possible to check the freewheel pawl spring condition by ear without taking the freewheel apart, well worth doing before any long trip. European freewheels have odd numbers of internal ratchet teeth, so that only one pawl is engaged at a time—but each ratchet tooth is engaged once by each pawl every revolution. Regina freewheels have 21 ratchet teeth, so that you should hear 42 clicks per revolution as you turn it backwards. Maillard have 13 and you should hear 26. Japanese freewheels have an even number of teeth, usually 16, and both pawls should engage at once. As you turn the freewheel backwards very slowly you should be able to hear a very slight double click at each ratchet tooth position as first one and then the second pawls engage. This check is most easily carried out turning the freewheel backwards by hand with the wheel out of the bicycle.

Brake blocks

It is best to buy, in the early stages of your cycling career at least, replacement blocks and shoes as a unit. There are basically two types of fitting: one has a plain rod about 5mm in diameter fixed at right angles to the shoe—this type is used by Mafac Racer centre-pulls, and Mafac and Dia-Compe cantilevers; the other type has a threaded portion instead which fits through a slot on nearly every other brake type and is secured by a nut. The brake shoe will be either closed at both ends, in which case you can fit it either way round, or closed at one end, in which case the closed end must face forwards. Single-ended shoes usually reinforce the point with an arrow pointing in the forward direction. Since the new brake block will be thicker than the old one you will probably have to readjust the cable via the clamp bolt. Make sure that all other adjusters are at their shortest screwed-down position before you do this.

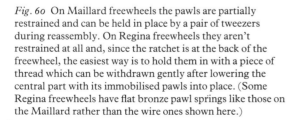

Fig. 60 On Maillard freewheels the pawls are partially restrained and can be held in place by a pair of tweezers during reassembly. On Regina freewheels they aren't restrained at all and, since the ratchet is at the back of the freewheel, the easiest way is to hold them in with a piece of thread which can be withdrawn gently after lowering the central part with its immobilised pawls into place. (Some Regina freewheels have flat bronze pawl springs like those on the Maillard rather than the wire ones shown here.)

Brake and gear cables

Replace wires as soon as they show the slightest sign of fraying or grating in use. It is generally best to replace the outer casing of brake cables at the same time. Cut the outer casing to length using pliers or wire cutters, without crimping the end coil. Undo the cable bolt at the brake or gear end and pull the wire right through. Keep any ferrules which fit over the ends of the outer casing (you may need to cut the plastic coating of the casing back wth a sharp blade to refit these). Note how the solder nipple of the inner wire is held at the lever end and then push the nipple out and remove the wire completely. Fit the nipple of the new wire in the same way and thread the wire through the lever parts. Smear the inner wire lightly with grease and put a small blob on the end of the outer casing so that the wire will carry it through. Push the wire right through the casing and any hangers and so on, finally clamping it again at the brake or gear end. Then, in the case of brake cables, put the brake on hard. This will test whether it is tightly clamped at the brake end and will also bed down the outer casing; you may well have to readjust and take up some more slack after this.

Parking and locking

You can avoid quite a lot of potential damage to your bicycle by taking care how and where you park it. A laden bicycle is a lot less stable than an unladen one.

Two absolute 'don'ts': never prop the machine up against the kerb by a pedal—it needs only a gust of wind, a careless passer-by or a car too close, for it to fall over. And never lean it with the top tube against a post; it can slip down or swing round.

Official parking places and cycle racks vary enormously. The common concrete slots should be avoided. Maybe in theory a $1\frac{1}{2}$in wheel will fit solid; in practice any lightweight wheel will bend. The vertical metal V-shaped racks common in shopping centres are slightly better but still unsuitable for loaded bikes. Better to look for a suitable wall or a Sheffield Stand.

Safest is to lean the bicycle firmly against a solid wall or railings. Lean it in at about five degrees to the vertical for stability, supported at both ends and preferably with the chain and gear side towards the wall. It should never be left where it could cause an obstruction. In the country it is often safest—in the absence of anything solid to lean it against—to lay it down; at least it won't fall over. Leave the gear and chain uppermost to avoid getting dirt and foliage in the works.

The best insurance against theft is to leave the

Fig. 61 The Sheffield cycle stand, the only type thoroughly approved by the CTC and cycle campaign groups. Note the tough U-shape lock on the left-hand bicycle (and the ouch! saddle on the other)

bicycle either locked away indoors or where you can see it. If you cannot keep it in sight then lock it and make it pilferproof.

No lock is proof against a determined and well-equipped professional thief. Even the fanciest locks can be broken with the right approach or the right equipment. What you *can* hope to do is to make the act of removing the machine so awkward, time-consuming and conspicuous that it's not worth the effort. Don't rely on the public intervening if they see somebody tampering with the lock. I know several cyclists who, having lost the key to a lock, have borrowed hacksaws and the like and gaily sawn away without any question being asked.

The first requirement is a good lock: the modern U-shaped type are definitely the strongest but are limited in what they can be fixed to. Some stout chain-fixing locks are also quite effective. If it's any good it's going to be bulky and heavy. The second requirement is something to lock the bicycle to. Stout railings are the best followed by a variety of poles and items of street furniture. If you have quick-release hubs you should make sure that both wheels are locked to the frame; this is about the only occasion when quick-release hubs show any disadvantage. Don't leave easily removable pumps, bottles, lights and bags on an unattended bicycle.

There's a world of difference between leaving a bicycle for ten minutes outside a sub-Post Office in the Western Highlands and leaving it for a whole day in central London. You will have to decide when it is necessary to take full precautions and when not. In towns leave the bicycle in a prominent position, rather than down an obscure side alley.

It is usually possible to obtain an 'all-risks' extension to a household policy to insure a bicycle or bicycles, but you should examine carefully what is covered, where—geographically—it is covered, what recompense you will receive if the machine is stolen and what special conditions are imposed. Cycle insurance on its own and not as part of a household policy is not easy to find nowadays; the CTC is one of the few organisations able to offer this to its members.

If you are unfortunate enough to lose a bicycle it is essential that you should be able to give an accurate description of it. It is worth noting the details of the principal components—and the frame number, usually stamped either on the left-hand rear fork end or underneath the bottom bracket. In several parts of the country schemes have been started for marking bicycles, again by stamping under the bottom bracket, with the post-code of the owner. Post-codes identify up to about a dozen households; all that needs to be added is the number or initials of the name of the individual dwelling. Such precautions are useful if a bicycle has been 'borrowed' by somebody who needed to be somewhere else quickly and then probably abandoned it—an endemic happening in such places as Oxford and Cambridge. They are, however, unlikely to be of much help if the bicycle is stolen by those who make a business of it and reassemble the components into different machines. Nevertheless, a substantial number of stolen bicycles are recovered by the police but never claimed, so it is worthwhile being persistent.

TWELVE

ROADSIDE REPAIRS

It is almost inevitable that you will at some time have to undertake some repair by the roadside. You can lengthen the odds by a few simple checks on your maintenance before you leave.

Tyres Check that the outer cover is not too worn, has no sidewall cuts to be patched, and that small flints, thorns etc, are no longer stuck in any of the inevitable small cuts in the tread.

Cables Check for any sign of fraying at the lever, or grating when the brake is applied or gears changed. Check both block and shoe for wear. Clean out any grit or metal swarf from the braking surface. Check that no part of the block touches the tyre.

Spokes Not much that you can do, I'm afraid, except to check that they are all intact and reasonably tight, and that the wheel is true.

Freewheels Check for general condition, including pawl engagement as given in Chapter 11. The best check for a freewheel is a quick ride round the houses, listening for noises as given in the next section of this chapter.

Bolts Should be checked for tightness, particularly chainring bolts, mudguard bolts, toeclip bolts, carrier fittings, brake lever fittings, brake fittings.

Chain Check for cleanliness, lubrication and noise.

Gear mechanism Clean and lubricate. Check that it doesn't touch spokes in bottom gear, nor throw the chain off in top.

Lights Check that bulbs and batteries (if used) are in working order.

Toeclips and straps Check that neither is so worn that it is likely to break. Toeclips usually break eventually just at the sharp bend in front of the pedal or at the similar bend beneath the toe — one side goes first, so look for cracks.

Major bearings Check that these are correctly adjusted and lubricated.

Irritating noises

Bicycle noises are irritating. They can be quite trivial in origin, or they can be warnings of a deeper malaise. Any sudden noise means: stop immediately and check.

The first characteristic of a noise is the frequency of its occurrence. If it happens once per wheel revolution, then it concerns a wheel, tyre, freewheel or mudguard. If it occurs once per pedal revolution, it concerns pedals, cranks, chainwheels, bottom bracket bearing or something in your trouser pocket. If it occurs once per complete chain circulation—from every four pedal revs on a small chainring to every two and a bit on the large—it concerns the chain. If it is continuous or irregular it can be gears or almost anything else. All bicycle noises are subject to the provisions of Sod's Law and may occur only under load, or inexplicably not under load, intermittently and only when your companion is not listening for them.

Rattles are generally the result of a fastening coming loose. Mudguards and carriers are the first suspects, followed by objects in the bag.

Knocking noises of wheel frequency are likely to be from the freewheel. If there is any looseness of the bearing, in certain gears (usually next to, and second from, top) some freewheels rock. The cure is to remove packing shims from inside the freewheel to tighten its bearings. Knocking noises at pedal frequency may be pedal bearings in need of adjustment, loose toeclip fixings or loose chainring bolts. Knocking at chain frequency is usually a tight link in the chain, less frequently a broken sideplate or chain roller.

Squeals from the brakes, if acute, are caused by oil or grease on the rim and by the blocks not being toed-in if chronic. Get advice before you attempt to bend the brake arm in by the necessary degree or two: it's not possible on some brakes. Grossly loose bearings may squeak; you should have noticed the looseness long before they get to that state. Scraping noises from the brake are particles of grit or metal caught in a brake block: dig them out quickly, otherwise they can score the rim.

Creaks at pedal frequency may be wear on the pedal plate rivets: with most makes you can gently peen them over with a ball pane hammer. The noise may also stem from a source as innocent as shoes and toestraps, or from the cranks, usually as a result of slight looseness or grease on the taper fitting to the bottom bracket axle. Take apart, clean and reassemble dry. Bars and stems sometimes creak for no reason, sometimes when they've been out in the wet and have corroded minutely where they are clamped, very rarely because they're cracked. Check immediately if a creak comes on suddenly. Saddles also sometimes creak for no better reason that spite, sometimes because one side of the clamp on the seat pillar is slightly loose, again very rarely if the saddle frame is cracked.

Crackling noises of any frequency or continuously indicate broken or damaged balls or bearing surfaces in hub, bottom bracket, pedal or freewheel bearings. Bottom bracket and pedal noises stop when you stop pedalling.

Rubbing noises, at wheel frequency or regularly two or three times per wheel revolution are usually a sign that the tyre is touching the frame or mudguard. The wheel may have pulled over to one side, the rear quick-release or track nuts may not be sufficiently tightened, a mudguard stay may have become bent or a defect may have developed in the tyre and the bulge is touching something. The regular bumping should also be obvious. Check immediately if it comes on suddenly. A milder rubbing noise may result from a leaf or twig under the mudguard or a brake block touching a rim through imperfect centring.

A regular soft click at wheel frequency may indicate that something is stuck in the tyre. It may be a small stone adhering, perhaps by tar or mud, or a sharp object may have penetrated the tyre. If you're quick enough you can catch it before it gets as far as the inner tube. Be circumspect: paradoxically if a fine thorn is sticking in and a dab of saliva on the hole shows that it is leaking air very slowly, then it may be better to leave it plugging the hole until you can change the tube in comfort. Thorns can sometimes be amazingly effective plugs.

A harp-like rapid pinging noise usually means that something is touching the spokes, often a strap from a bag, or possibly a small twig caught in the mudguard.

Puncture repair

Punctures rank with rain, hills and saddle soreness in the outside world's litany of cycling tragedies they would hope to be spared. Here, however, is the truth.

All puncture repairs are much easier with the wheel removed from the bicycle, and in any case for tube changes you have to take the wheel out. Quick-release hubs certainly save a lot of fiddling. Pump the tyre up and see if you can hear where air is escaping; if you can, note the position relative to the valve or lettering on the tyre wall so that you can check when the tube is out whether the cause of the puncture is still sticking through the tyre—and whether the outer cover needs to be patched as well.

Always carry at least one spare inner tube, so that you don't have to cope with trying to stick patches onto a wet punctured tube in the dark in a downpour (the sort of conditions that punctures naturally choose). With a spare tube the stages covered by pictures 5 to 11 are bypassed while you're actually on the road and can be carried out in comfort—and without having to hurry—at home.

Getting the tyre off Let the tyre down completely and remove the knurled locking ring (if fitted) that holds the valve stem square to the rim (Fig. 62.1). Push the spoon end of the first tyre lever gently under the tyre wire, either near the puncture if you've found it and intend to mend the tube, or near the valve if you are going to remove the whole tube (Fig. 62.2). You are only going to remove one side of the tyre, so take care that the lever is under only the tyre edge on your side. On a rear wheel take the tyre off from the side opposite the freewheel block.

You will find that cyclists who offer you advice are sharply divided into those who start taking a tyre off and finish putting it on *at* the valve, and those who start and finish *opposite* it. With a loose-fitting tyre it doesn't matter a lot, but with a tight one, finishing putting it on at the valve is appreciably easier, because the tyre wires opposite can bed down further. This is also the recommendation of the tyre manufacturers. Be gentle with tyre levers; makers of the flexible-bead lightweight tyres supply plastic ones which are easier on their tyres. In any case levers should be free of sharp edges. In dire emergency you can use the handles of spoons or forks; in even direr emergency we've twice had to use tyre levers to spread butter and jam.

Hook the notch in the first lever—if it has one— round a convenient spoke; hold it down with your spare hand if it hasn't. Then insert the second lever about 7cm (3in) away from the first (Fig. 62.3), and repeat with a third lever if necessary until a long enough piece of the tyre wire is over the edge of the rim for you to take the rest off by hand.

At this stage—and indeed any time you have a tyre off the rim, for whatever reason—feel round the inside of the outer cover (Fig. 62.4) to check whether anything sharp is sticking through. Be careful: if it's

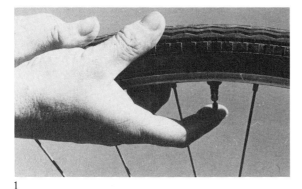

1

2

3

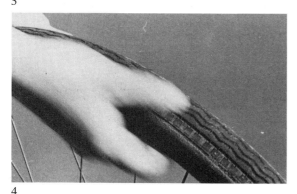

4

sharp enough to get through a tyre or tube it could be sharp enough to cut your finger. If there is anything, remove it by pushing it out from the inside to avoid enlarging the hole.

Mending the tube Pump it up lightly, say ten strokes of the hand pump. Listen carefully round it for air escaping; another bizarre-sounding—and looking—but a very effective method is to hold the tube close to the sensitive surface of the upper lip, where you can often feel the minute jet of escaping air even if it's too quiet to hear. You can confirm the spot with a little dab of saliva. Alternatively immerse the tube in sections in water, moving it round and looking for the tell-tale stream of bubbles (Fig. 62.5).

Dry the tube thoroughly if you've used the water test or if it's a wet day, and then clean the area round the hole with sandpaper or emery cloth (Fig. 62.6). Failure to make patches stick firmly is almost always because this stage hasn't been carried out properly. Clean off surface dirt *and* the slightly glossy sheen of the rubber until it's a matt black (or red or rubber colour as appropriate). Make sure you clean an area rather bigger than the size of patch you're using. You don't need to use very big patches for flint or thorn holes: the ones about 15mm across are quite adequate.

Then apply a thinnish coat of rubber solution to the

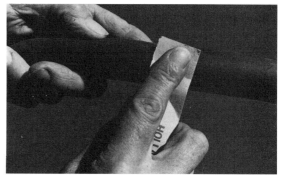

5

6

7

8

9

10

11

12

13

14

Fig. 62 Puncture repair sequence

cleaned area and spread it, too, to cover an area larger than the patch (Fig. 62.7). On black butyl rubber tubes allow this first coat of rubber solution to dry and then apply a second coat and allow that to dry too. Red and natural coloured tubes need only one coat. The bonding process is a chemical one and has nothing to do with the coated area being sticky. Let the solution dry completely: this takes from a minute upwards depending on air temperature.

Select your patch and remove its protective foil backing (occasionally it's a waxed linen instead) to expose the adhesive side: don't touch this surface (Fig. 62.8). Press the patch firmly into position, taking particular care to smooth down the edges (Fig. 62.9). Remove the backing paper by pinching the patch so that the paper tears across the middle (Fig. 62.10); you can then take the paper off from the centre outwards without risking lifting the edges of the patch. Use feather-edge patches (German Rema Tip-Top is among the best); not only do they make a neater job but if necessary you can also repair holes quite close to other earlier patches (Fig. 62.11).

Putting the tyre back on The manufacturers recommend dusting the tube lightly with french chalk (talcum powder works too). Inflate the tube slightly, about four pump strokes. Then put the valve through the hole in the rim and nestle the tube evenly into the outer cover (Fig. 62.12). Begin to replace the cover by rolling the tyre wire over the rim opposite the valve. Use your thumbs to roll it on (Fig. 62.13) from the side that you're trying to mount; don't try to pull it on from the other side. Continue to roll it on, working round the rim in both directions until there is about a 15–20cm (6–8in) length left bridging the valve. This will feel quite tight and you may begin to despair about getting it on at all. Let all the air out of the tube and roll the length of tyre edge that you have already got on right down into the well of the rim. Then roll the last section of tyre edge on (Fig. 62.14) with the base of the thumbs. Never use tyre levers to replace the tyre—it's the sort of breach of etiquette that gets a chap cashiered from his regiment. Anyway, it's unnecessary if you roll the edge on and don't pick at it from the wrong side.

Finally push the valve up to make sure that the valve base is above the tyre wires. Replace the outer knurled locknut and begin to pump the tyre up. Stop after about 15 strokes of the handpump or at about 1 bar (15psi) and check that the cover is on evenly by spinning the wheel. If it isn't, correct it (by using the same thumb rolling action) until the lines of the tyre moulding are the same distance above the rim all the way round. Then finish pumping up.

So, a mere puncture is not one of the great cycling disasters. Be sure, however, not to confuse a punctured tube with any unpunctured spare you have.

Major disasters

The remedies here for these rare happenings are drastic and designed only to get you home or to help.

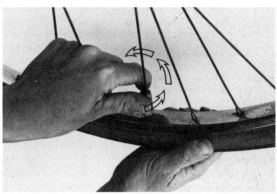

Fig. 63 Roadside spoke replacement. You can often get away without taking the tyre off—though you may have to remove the freewheel if a rear wheel spoke breaks on that side. To remove the broken spoke (which nearly always breaks at the head) unscrew in the direction shown. To tighten the replacement, turn the nipple key in the direction shown. As a rough-and-ready guide, tighten until the spoke feels about as taut as the adjacent ones

Badly buckled wheel Can often be made true enough to run between the forks by levering it back towards the right shape in a gate, fence or drain, or by laying it on the road and standing on the appropriate bits. Be very careful in using brakes.

Broken fork blade or crown Very rare nowadays in normal use and there is virtually nothing you can do except walk. It is dangerous in the extreme to attempt to ride a machine with any part of the front fork broken.

Broken fork column Usually leaves the machine dangerously unridable *unless* the break is at the top threaded portion, in which case it *may* be possible to bridge the break by putting the handlebar stem as far down as it will go into the fork column. This requires extreme care.

Broken frame tube or stay A broken top or down tube (also very rare) will generally make the machine unridable. A broken seat tube may allow you to freewheel gingerly, but cause everything to jam up when you apply pressure; the same goes for a broken chain or seat stay. You may be able to walk part and 'scoot', hobby-horse style, or freewheel. It may be helpful to lower the saddle.

Broken handlebar extension Leaves the machine unridable.

Broken handlebar bend Can be ridden, although not legally unless the unbroken side carries the front brake lever and you have a fixed wheel. Depending on the distance you have to cover, it may be worth swapping the front brake cable to the side remaining and riding in a wary fashion.

Freewheel freewheeling both ways This means that both pawl springs have broken or are gummed up; replace or try the following. Walk if necessary to a point where you can freewheel for a distance. Then, with the chain set to give you a reasonable gear for the rest of your journey, try pedalling once you have got up to a moderate speed—centrifugal force *may* push the pawls out against the ratchet. Once you have made one of them engage, then keep pedalling, against the force of the brake if necessary, and do not attempt to freewheel at any point. Pouring hot water over the freewheel may ungum stuck pawls but won't do the freewheel (or hub) much good.

Freewheel jammed Try riding very carefully. Any attempt at freewheeling or any lagging behind the road speed of the bicycle will wrap the gear mechanism up in the chain; or you can shorten the chain to bypass the gear.

Bent or broken rear gear mechanism Shorten the chain so that it will bypass the gear mechanism: use on whichever rear sprocket is in line with the middle chainring to give you a single gear.

Broken hub axle These almost always break at the inner end of the cone. By juggling spacers you may be able to move it so that both halves screw into the cone, meeting in the middle, which bridges the break. It won't take much loading so be gentle.

Broken seat pillar You may be able to jam a piece of wood to hold the two bits together, clamping the join by the frame seat bolt or, alternatively, lower the sadle and use what's left. This may leave you problems in getting the broken bit out.

Broken saddle frame or clip 'Honk'—also applicable to the preceding! (But even honking is not easy without a saddle.)

Broken carrier Strap it up with the ever-useful toe-straps or fashion one from a piece of wood as shown in Fig. 64. This will be strong enough to hold up a saddlebag but it won't take panniers.

Broken brake cable Obviously best replaced by the real thing but in an emergency it is possible to use a toestrap to tension the straddle wire of a centre-pull brake to the point where the other brake can be used for fine control.

Broken crank or pedal axle Tighten the toestrap so that you can pull up on the remaining pedal as well as pushing down and ride one-legged. Remember the exploits of Bernard Migaud and Hugh Culverhouse. *Your* biggest problem is likely to be where to put your spare foot to keep it out of the way of the broken crank. If the left crank breaks it may be easier to take it off.

Broken chain Shorten by two links using the chain tool. Don't use largest chainring or sprocket until you've checked that remaining length is sufficient.

Fig. 64 You can fashion a makeshift carrier from a piece of wood. Curve A fits against the rear of the seat tube; notches B and C fit against the seat stays, resting on the brake bridge

Badly gashed tyre outer cover If possible sew up or even staple across the cut. Then stick a substantial patch underneath: piece of denim, car inner tube, canvas, nylon. Or swathe the cover when it's off the rim in plastic insulating tape. Inflate just hard enough to prevent the rim bottoming on the road. Don't expect miracles. The stories about stuffing tyres with grass are apocryphal.

THIRTEEN

THE CYCLIST AND THE LAW

The Law

For a brief but heady spell in the 1880s, following the invention of the safety bicycle and the pneumatic tyre, the bicycle was the fastest vehicle on the road. But to claim to be King of the Road was to challenge the established order; worse, bicycles frightened the horses. Some local councils were therefore attempting to make, piecemeal, regulations to restrict cycling. But in 1883 the CTC was instrumental in thwarting these attempts by having the bicycle declared to be 'a carriage' under the Local Government Act. Ever since, it has been subject to national legislation.

Cyclists are said to be technically in charge of a vehicle—even though virtually all of the 1888 Act's provisions have been repealed or superseded bit by bit over the years.

As the law now stands, you *must*:

Before setting out, ensure that your cycle has efficient brakes. Two independent braking systems are required on a bicycle with wheels larger than 18in in diameter, one acting on each wheel. For the purposes of the Pedal Cycles (Construction and Use) Regulations 1983 a fixed wheel (direct drive without freewheel) counts at present as one braking system.

When riding your bicycle, and even when wheeling it, observe traffic signs and signals—including one-way directions and no right/left/U-turn indications, double white lines and yellow road markings (waiting restrictions)—and the directions of a police officer or traffic warden controlling traffic. You must also stop when required to do so by a school-crossing patrol or police officer in uniform.

Give way to ambulances, fire engines and mountain or cave rescue, coastguard or police vehicles with sirens sounding and blue lights flashing.

Whether wheeling or riding the bicycle, give precedence to pedestrians on 'zebra' or push-button controlled 'pelican' crossings.

When riding after dark, carry a front lamp showing a white light, a rear lamp bearing the British Standards Institution mark and the number 'BS 3648' showing a red light, and an approved rear reflector, such as one marked 'BS AU40 LI'. The red warnings must be attached to the machine on the centre line or offside, not more than 20in (50.8cm) from the rearmost part of the bicycle, and at a height from the ground of not more than 3ft 6in (106.7cm) nor less than 15in (38.1cm). These lamps are required to be visible 'from a reasonable distance'. The front lamp must now also be fixed on the centre line or offside. (These details of placing of lights apply to bicycles and tricycles with wheels greater than 18in in diameter; there are slightly different requirements for those with smaller wheels or with sidecars or trailers.)

A new bicycle sold by way of trade (i.e. by a dealer) and not designed specifically for competition must conform to BS6102: Part 1. The main provisions of the Standard concerning strength, projections and so on, though sometimes niggling, are unexceptionable. The more controversial points concern spoke-mounted reflectors—which must be fitted when the bicycle is sold—and the dictation of which brake must be connected to which brake lever position. You are at liberty to remove the spoke reflectors (which can have an unbalancing effect on the wheel) and swap the brakes once you have bought the machine, if you choose.

You *may not*:

Ride recklessly, without due care and attention, or without reasonable consideration for other persons using the road. (There used to be a splendid offence of 'riding furiously'. Sadly, it has now gone.)

Ride under the influence of drink or a drug. There is no statutory limit on blood alcohol concentration for the cyclist, nor any compulsion to submit to a test.

Hold onto a motor vehicle or trailer in motion on any road.

Carry a passenger unless your machine is 'constructed or adapted for the carriage of more than one person'.

Stop, except in an emergency to avoid an accident, on a pedestrian crossing, or leave your cycle where waiting is prohibited, or leave it on any road in such a way that it is likely to cause danger to other road users. Neither may you 'by negligence or misbehaviour interrupt the free passage of any road user or vehicle'.

Overtake the moving vehicle nearest the crossing nor pass the leading vehicle which has stopped to give way to a pedestrian on the approach to a 'zebra' crossing marked by zigzag white lines.

Wilfully ride on a 'footpath (footway) by the side of any road made or set apart for the use of foot-passengers'— that is, on what everybody except the law, highway engineers and Americans calls the 'pavement'—except to cross it for access.

Ride along a road designated as a motorway or on a road, path or area set aside for pedestrian use covered by a valid order prohibiting cycling and showing the appropriate signs.

You *may*:

After dark, without lamps, wheel your bicycle while on foot as near as possible to the left-hand edge of the carriageway, or stop in a similar position temporarily with lamps unlit while mounted to comply with traffic signals etc.

Ride in marked bus lanes where they flow with the normal direction of traffic and, where indicated, on certain 'contra-flow' lanes.

Ride on a bridleway or prescribed long-distance cross-country route with the obligation to give way when necessary to walkers and riders. The position on country footpaths is obscure: there is certainly neither blanket permission nor proscription and common-sense and courtesy should be observed.

The Highway Code

The Code has not the force of law, but breaches of it may be quoted as supporting evidence for charges, particularly in the ill-defined regions of recklessness, carelessness, danger or obstruction. The Highway Code exhorts you:

To make sure that your cycle is in good condition before you ride it.

Before starting off or turning right or left or pulling up, to glance behind to see that the manoeuvre is safe, and signal your intention.

Not to ride more than two abreast (or 'side-by-side' as the latest version coyly says, lest the word 'abreast' should rouse unquenchable passions) and to ride in single file on narrow busy roads.

Before turning right on a busy road to check that it may not be safer to pull into the left and wait for a gap in the traffic in both directions before crossing.

While riding, always to hold the handlebar and keep your feet on the pedals, not to hold onto another vehicle or cyclist, not to ride close behind another vehicle, not to carry anything which may affect your balance nor to lead an animal.

To wear light-coloured or reflective and fluorescent clothing.

To use a 'suitable' cycle path beside the road, if there is one.

Road signs

Road signs are designed to certain codes. Circular signs give orders, triangular ones warn, and rectangular inform. Blue discs give positive orders, red discs or circles prohibit or limit. There are exceptions: notably the inverted red-rimmed triangle 'Give Way' and the red octagonal 'Stop'. Both are mandatory.

While you must learn the meaning of all road signs, there are some which are specific to cyclists. The most important is the prohibitory 'No cycling' sign: a black bicycle outline on white in a red ring. The other signs are blue. These mark paths for cyclists' use only, paths for mixed pedestrian and cycle use, lanes for bus and cycle use, recommended cycle routes and cycle parking facilities.

Fig. 65 Triangular sizes warn, rectangular signs inform,
circular signs instruct . . .

FOURTEEN
RIDING TECHNIQUES

Getting on

Bicycle textbooks of the Victorian era used to contain detailed instructions for mounting. The correct way hasn't changed much: you should step through an open frame—or raise your leg over the top tube of the diamond one—and place the right foot in its proper place on the pedal, which should be in line with the down tube. Scooting along and then swinging your leg over the saddle is unstable while you're doing it and puts unnecessary sideways stresses on the bicycle.

Having checked that the road behind is clear, accelerate by pushing down with the right foot and bringing the left one onto its pedal. The art of picking up the second pedal when using toestraps is easier to acquire than to describe. The weight of the clip and strap ensures that the pedal is always upside down when you put your foot on it. A light backwards movement of the foot turns the pedal over so that the front inch or two of the shoe goes into the gap between the toeclip and strap and the correct surface of the pedal. A deft wiggle then slips the foot fully home. Practise this on a stretch of quiet road until it becomes second nature and learn to do it with either foot, without looking down. Toestraps should be moderately tight; having them tighter helps pedalling, particularly uphill, but you will also have to learn to flip the quick-release buckles loose as you stop.

Riding

A properly designed bicycle which is in track should be almost self-steering. Riding hands-off is a very sensitive test of the alignment of a frame. Leaning the bicycle gently into the corner, putting more weight on the outside pedal makes steering nearly automatic. Lift the pedal on the inside of the corner to increase ground clearance (if using a freewheel, that is); this avoids grounding the pedal on the inside—always unnerving and potentially dangerous.

The bicycle is less stable when cornering, subject to sideways forces, than when going straight, so avoid actions, such as braking, which further test the grip of the tyre at the same time. Slippery surfaces are much more objectionable when cornering; surmounting small obstructions is more difficult at an acute angle of approach. Cross hazards of this type—railway lines at level crossings, metal plates and covers, raised road markings, low kerbs at laybys and entrances—as nearly as possible at right angles and upright, especially when it is wet.

Care can surprisingly reduce the risk of punctures. Avoid glass from broken bottles, car lamps etc by spotting the tell-tale glint well ahead. Fortunately windscreen glass breaks into less jagged little cubes. In the country, outside the flinty chalk hill country of south and south-east England, the worst puncture hazard is hedge clippings, usually hawthorn or blackthorn. Be wary when you see signs of recent hedge trimming: stop immediately if you hear the rhythmic tick of something in the tyre.

Stopping

The *front* brake does the stopping and slowing down. Decelerating throws the effective line of action of your weight forward, so that more of it acts on the front wheel. This means that the rear brake is relatively ineffective on deceleration. However, if you use the front brake violently you could move your weight so far forward that you go right over the top—though you would have to be very clumsy indeed to do this on a laden touring bicycle. Gentleness and smoothness are the essence of all riding techniques. On slippery surfaces—a just-wet road after a dry spell, oil patches, leaves, loose gravel, mud, metal road furniture, level-crossing rails—careless slamming on of either brake can induce a skid, with the rear brake this can happen even on a dry smooth road. Then the bicycle slews either from side to side or away entirely to one side. A front-wheel skid in slippery conditions could put you on the ground. So, gentleness is everything. Sum up the road ahead and brake *before* bends or hazards.

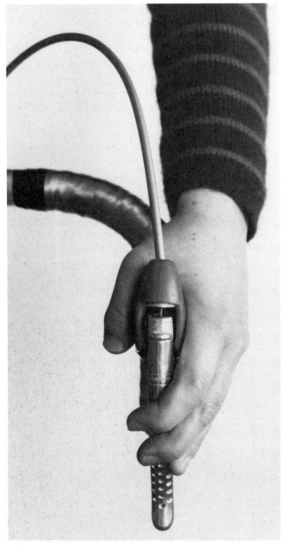

Fig. 66 Applying the brake from the on-the-hoods position—useful in group riding, in traffic and on mountain descents

first two or three fingers together down the length of the lever. This wrist action is perhaps a little less natural than the conventional one but the technique is very effective for gentle control of speed and even for major stopping when you get used to it. It is near essential in city traffic. Its main advantage on long downhills is that the more upright position offers more wind resistance and automatically limits your speed. Obviously body weight and size influence this, but I find that there is very little need to use brakes at all—except for sharp corners—on gradients up to about 8 per cent (1-in-12).

In an emergency you may have to use both brakes hard together to stop. If you're on a bend, concentrate on stopping, not on cornering. Fortunately it is instinctive to tense your arms and to push your body backwards, which helps to keep the back wheel down. After any major skid check the tyre.

Brakes are much less effective in the wet—stopping distances can be many times greater than with dry rims. Dry off the rim by applying the brake long before it is needed to remove the thin water film from the rim surface. Chromium-plated steel rims need more braking heat to warm up and are intrinsically more slippery. There are now special wet-weather brake blocks specific to different rim materials (and sometimes less effective in the dry than normal ones). A soft rubber block on aluminium alloy is still as good as any. But the key is still to know exactly what the performance of your brakes is in the wet, to ride within it and to cultivate the balance between front and rear.

Taking the rough . . .

Sadly, Britain's (more particularly England's) road surfaces—and often on the minor roads that cyclists use—are deteriorating. Some local authorities now deliberately spend less of their maintenance budgets on minor roads. Often traffic far heavier than these roads were intended to bear has cracked the foundations or 'widened' the road by eroding the verges or banks. Rough patches and potholes, augmented by poorly filled-in service trenches, are commonplace and you have to learn to deal with them (including reporting them; highway authorities have a statutory duty not to leave their roads strewn with holes).

On a completely traffic-free road you can avoid most obstacles, by moving out and back in smoothly. But at other times, for example at trenches that cross the road, you must learn to ease yourself over them (and over cattle-grids in open country). Sitting up in either of the on-the-tops positions and *pulling* at the bars naturally transfers your weight from the saddle to your

The main purpose of the rear brake is not for slowing down but to hold speed steady on downhill stretches where this is desirable, and to supplement the front brake where necessary. Braking on a long downhill can heat the rims up—enough at the extreme to 'lift' repair patches on the inner tubes. Share the heat dissipation between the wheels, by putting conscious emphasis on the back brake. A suddenly flat front tyre is more difficult to control than a rear.

It is very useful to learn to apply brakes from the 'on-the-hoods' position. This involves pressing with the

Fig. 67 Sadly many of Britain's roads are deteriorating, particularly at the edges where cyclists ride

Fig. 68 Beware the innocent-looking puddle: it may have hidden depths, and a sharp edge on the far shore

legs—which should both be bent, with the cranks near the quarter-to-three horizontal position. The bicycle then 'rides' the rough patch without transferring the bumps to you. Cattle grids and roughness with no sharp edges are best taken at normal speed at right angles, without braking while you're crossing.

Potholes with sharp edges call for more care. Skilled cyclo-cross riders and road racers can actually jump a bicycle over small obstacles—less easy with a laden machine. The technique is to give a sharp pull on the bars from the on-the-hoods position as you come to the sharp edge, just lifting the front wheel off the ground. Once it's past the bump, transfer your weight forward, bend both knees simultaneously to try to lift the back wheel to reduce the weight on it as it crosses the ridge. Even on a loaded bicycle you will lessen any impact and avoid the main cause of damage at potholes—impacting the front rim on the far edge. Tyres of fatter section make it all much easier. You do need to slow for bad obstacles of this kind. It is particularly useful to be able to do this little jump in town traffic where you can't go round a hole.

Fig. 69 Sometimes you can't avoid an obstruction such as this badly-restored trench but there's often a line *(arrowed)* between trough and hump which is nearly level

Using the gears

Derailleur gearing defies all sorts of engineering rules but nevertheless works. The early car designer who said deprecatingly of his new gearbox *'C'est brutal mais ça marche'* ('it's barbaric, but it works') had obviously never encountered the derailleur gear.

For most types there are no definite indicated markings or click-settings for the rear gear's five or six positions. Top and bottom are limited by the adjustment stops, but intermediate ones have to be found by feel. The chain has to be moving at a reasonable speed, so don't try to change below about 50rpm. Don't leave changing too late on a hill. Keep the pedals turning but ease the *pressure* on them momentarily, particularly uphill. Move the lever briskly slightly beyond the position required and then flick it minutely back to the right place. If you've got it wrong the chain makes a noise: a clanking against a larger sprocket (move the lever slightly forwards) or grating as it rides up and tries to change to a smaller one (slightly backwards). Explosive noises and jumping mean you've left it much too late. With practice changes can be made almost silently. Derailleur gears will *not* change when you are stationary or freewheeling.

The front changer has two basic extreme positions; the middle one you have to find by feel. It may be necessary to trim the adjustment on the front gear after changing the back one to compensate for the different chain line. The chain drops more readily from a larger ring to a smaller one, than it climbs to larger sprockets at the back. By remaining on the big or middle ring for most riding and only changing to the small one for the very hard bits you have this emergency drop in hand most of the time. On the way back up again, the reverse change is best carried out when you are pedalling briskly. Although it is normal to operate the rear gear lever with the right hand and the front one with the left, it is worth learning to move either lever with either hand if necessary. There is rarely any need to change both together or in quick succession with the gearing set-up suggested in Chapter 3; just treat them as 'easy',

'medium' and 'hard' sets. You *don't* go through every gear of your 15 or 18 in numerical sequence.

Everybody has differing capabilities and natural rhythms uphill. Natural fast climbing is a born gift and one prized in racing circles. Outstanding climbers are usually very lightly built and earn from the Continental press such honorifics as the 'Eagle of Toledo' or the 'Angel of the Mountains'. Their rivals consider their wings unfair.

For comfort, not speed, variable gears enable you to maintain a relatively close range of pedalling speeds irrespective of the road speed dictated by conditions. There is no 'correct' gear for a particular hill: there is an appropriate gear for a given rider on a particular day in a particular state of fitness or fatigue. Use the gears to keep your own human motor turning happily. Give yourself time to change down.

On any occasion, then, every cycle-tourist will have a 'natural' climbing speed and will find it irksome to go much slower and uncomfortable to attempt to go much faster. If you are climbing in company it is better to fix a rendezvous at the top—or at intervals on a long climb—rather than break your natural rhythm.

Steady in-the-saddle climbing is usually most comfortable in the transverse 'on-the-tops' position, which gives your diaphragm a bit of extra space. You will also find it easier if you pull lightly on the bars. In mountain country you have to develop a kind of fatalistic patience: hurry is out.

Wind is a quite different obstacle. All that you can do is to make your frontal area as small as possible (the 'on-the-drops' position) and not be too proud to change down to a gear which may seem absurdly low for the flat. Side winds can be nearly as hard to deal with as head ones. Shelter is one way of avoiding wind: it's much easier riding in someone else's 'wind shadow' and sharing the effort between you with turns at the front. Also it helps to choose a potentially sheltered route (Chapter 16).

Finally, learn to change down for junctions or before stopping, so that you will be in the right gear for moving smoothly away.

FIFTEEN

RIDING IN TRAFFIC

Bicycles and cyclists are fragile and vulnerable by comparison with other traffic. But there are times when you *have* to share the road with more motor vehicles than you would choose. There are techniques and rules which can help—but first a few principles.

Throughout you must ride positively but defensively, be prepared for other people's mistakes, know your rights—and recognise when it's just not practical to insist, when it's time to give way rather than hit anything or be hit.

Most drivers are reasonable people—although, as with cyclists, there will be the forgetful, the intolerant and the clueless among them. And there will probably be a deep ignorance of what it's actually like out there on a bike. All your moves must be expected by other road users: you must be predictable to the point of dullness.

You too must be reasonable in your expectations and behaviour. You should not cause unreasonable obstruction; there's no point in parking yourself in front of a Porsche when the road ahead is clear. It is *not* unreasonable, though, to occupy enough of a short narrow space past, say, roadworks or a parked vehicle to ensure that nobody is going to attempt to elbow past where there isn't room. Your overall aim is to complete your journey expeditiously and safely, not to prove that the bicycle is the fastest vehicle on the road (which, in many circumstances, it is).

Fig. 70 Don't ignore traffic lights

You *must* obey road signs and traffic lights. Traffic lights are the cyclist's friend. Over the first 50 metres a bicycle can be as fast as anything else, which gives you a better chance of merging into the traffic stream. Traffic lights also create a little haven where you can cross busy roads safely. A distressingly high proportion of urban cyclists seem to ignore traffic lights; there seems to be a quite widespread myth that cyclists may filter left through a red light (probably arising from the fact that the comparable manoeuvre is permissible in some states of the USA). As far as Britain is concerned it is indeed a myth, and a dangerous one: if there's a filter arrow or a cut-off bypassing the lights you can filter—if not, you can't. An even more dangerous myth—fortunately less widespread—is that traffic lights don't apply to cyclists at all. They do. When the lights turn to amber be prepared to stop—but check what any car behind you is doing. If the lights go amber as you're crossing, sprint!

You *must* give way to pedestrians on zebra or pelican (light-controlled) crossings: not only is it illegal not to, it is immoral to terrorise pedestrians by methods you would despise motorists for using on you. No right- or left-turn signs and one-way streets (except for marked contra-flow lanes) apply to you too. Turning past a 'No entry' sign or riding the wrong way down a one-way street are the pinnacles of unexpected behaviour. Some schemes may seem arbitrary and dotty: the answer is agitation and political pressure, not ignoring them. Do not ride along the pavement (footway) beside the road; it is an offence and it is offensive. On shared pedestrian-cycle paths ride at a human speed—be tolerant of the very young, the very old and the handicapped. Don't be the trigger for an explosion which demolishes in seconds the patient efforts of those who have spent years working on behalf of cyclists.

An on-the-drops riding position is not appropriate

in heavy traffic: you have got to be able to see what is going on around you—over a far wider circle than is offered by any mirror. You must cultivate the rapid glance behind, over or under either shoulder. It's almost essential to be able to apply the brakes from the on-the-hoods position. If you're doing enough town riding, there could be advantages in having a special town bicycle with flat bars with the brakes readily to hand. An interesting configuration would be the inverted handlebar style used on 'low-profile' time-trial bicycles, but of course placed higher up.

You must have every mechanical confidence in your machine, particularly in acceleration and stopping. For that reason many experienced town riders use a bicycle with a single gear, usually in the low sixties. Some go further and use a single fixed gear for reaction time and enhanced stopping power. If you are using derailleur gears make sure that they're definitely engaged before you move off. Fatter tyres offer advantages in traffic where it is impossible to go round small bumps and drains. Double-sided pedals, for a sure foot grip even out of the clips, are desirable for town riding.

Any urban journey should avoid hazardous spots as far as possible and should also avoid taking in roads on which traffic expects to move very fast.

There are two ways of riding in traffic. The best, if you are strong and confident enough, and if the traffic

Fig. 71 A diagrammatic representation of the wind created by heavy vehicles. A lorry, or bus has a marked bow wave and others from other parts depending on shape and speed, which tend to push a cyclist in towards the kerb. There can also be eddies round cabs, trailers and wheels. Behind the vehicle there is a large zone of often quite violent turbulence—which can stretch back 50 or 100 metres—which tends to suck the rider out towards the middle of the road. This is especially unpleasant if a succession of lorries is passing, with a corresponding succession of left-right buffetings

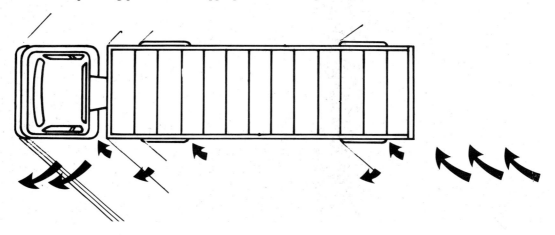

is moving at a reasonable speed (usually 25 to 40kph, 16 to 25mph), is to make yourself part of the traffic stream. This is usually practicable up to the point where the traffic is moving 20-25kph faster than you are, and enables you to take up the correct lane, or the correct part of it, for your next move. You gain a clearer view of how traffic is flowing and see potential obstructions or hazards well ahead. You have to be aware what traffic is doing on both sides of you, as well as behind and in front. Sometimes the traffic will be too fast for you and you will just have to follow the second method; others may prefer to do this all the time. It consists of sticking basically to the left-hand edge of the road and so merely having to be wary of traffic which may encroach on your preserve. This needs particular care at junctions where you want to go straight on but others may wish to go left. It also leaves you coping with parked vehicles and the debris that accumulates near the kerb.

One other urban hazard you must be prepared for is sudden wind buffeting from unexpected directions. This occurs when wind is reflected, deflected and channelled by buildings; it is often worst where two city 'canyons' between tall blocks intersect.

Fig. 72 This cyclist knows that she doesn't want to go left with the left-hand traffic stream, so she's waiting for the lights in the correct position in the straight-ahead lane

Techniques and rules

In dense traffic you have to ride with precision, often in a narrow corridor, maybe only a metre wide. Your judgement of width has to be instinctive, like a cat's, so don't have bags or handlebars that jut out appreciably beyond the easily-judged body width.

You must be able to ride very slowly at times, even sit stationary for a few seconds. A single fixed gear makes this easier. There will often not be room to avoid drain covers and the unkempt trappings of the gutter; ease yourself over them.

Hold your lane—don't switch around. Only move from lane to lane to get ready for a turn, and then only in the traffic stream or when everything is stationary. Most of the time the direction you intend to go in should be obvious from your position; if it isn't, check behind and signal in good time. Look directly at, and catch the eye of, whoever you're signalling to if you can. A signal is an indication of what you wish to do: it does not automatically make your proposed manoeuvre instantly possible. A signal is worthless without the quick check behind first.

At any junction know where you want to go—and be in the correct lane, or even the appropriate part of the correct lane. Don't block a left filter lane if you don't want to go left. If you are not sure of your way stop and get off the road (if you can do it without

causing problems to anybody else) or follow the lane that you are in until you can stop, and then sort it out. Don't dither in the junction while you make up your mind.

Roundabouts illustrate the cyclist's perpetual dilemma. The rules are clear enough: you take up the appropriate lane as you enter—left if you're taking the first exit, otherwise centre or offside depending on the layout and your destination; you give way to traffic already on the roundabout; when it's clear you follow the lane as far as the exit before yours, then filter and signal left as you approach your exit. This is fine if you are fast and confident enough, or the traffic slow enough, for you to join the stream. The smaller the roundabout, the more traffic has to slow down and the easier your task. Mini-roundabouts, in effect simple or multiple junctions with priority to traffic coming from the right, offer few problems. It is very large roundabouts on trunk roads with fast-moving traffic that are difficult. The Highway Code advice—that you may find it easier to get off and walk across each exit individually until you reach the one you want—while defeatist, and quite wrong in principle, may on occasion be the only practicable solution. Many such roundabouts now have lanes marked for particular routes or destinations and some have anomalous 'Give way' lines—that is, not conforming to the 'priority-to-traffic-from-the-right' convention. Be wary.

In a few places, mostly in towns, these large roundabouts are being converted into festoons of mini-roundabouts. Despite the bizarre appearance (the first one, at Hemel Hempstead, quickly earned the local name of 'The Magic Roundabout') the concept, which allows two-way traffic both ways round the system, works well and is much easier for the cyclist.

Be conspicuous in your positioning. All vehicles have blind spots behind pillars and so on. Don't creep into a place where a lorry or van driver can't possibly see you.

Don't go up a stationary traffic queue and then stop on the left of a vehicle that's signalling a left turn. If you're going left you stand a good chance of being squeezed into the kerb; if you're not going left you should be on the other side of the vehicle.

In heavy and sluggish traffic—less than bicycle pace—there's more room between lanes one and two, or two and three, than between lane one and the kerb. There are also likely to be fewer people stepping off the kerb in front of you (though don't bank on it: I once met a jogger going the wrong way up the third lane of London's Euston Road).

Don't go into a closing gap. You should be able to tell from the way the front wheels are pointing whether vehicles in front of you, moving or stationary, are converging. You are obviously safer in narrow gaps between stationary vehicles than between moving ones. Beware of entering gaps between slowly moving long high-sided vehicles: the gap may disappear before you get to the front.

Expect drivers to make sudden and often unsignalled changes of plan in heavy traffic as they see one of the other lanes apparently moving faster than theirs. They probably won't have the slightest idea that they have incommoded you and should of course be fried in boiling oil for inattention—but in an imperfect world you have to let them go.

Expect taxis and buses to stop to pick up fares. Don't ride on the left of a bus unless you're sure you're going to turn left before the next stop. Taxis are driven by professionals whom I have nearly always found very considerate to cyclists, particularly if the cyclists appear to know what they're doing. Cyclists often don't realise that taxis will be driven like bicycles: if there's a taxi-sized gap, a taxi will go into it.

Use every scrap of available evidence to check the position and movements of other vehicles. Keep an eye on reflections in shop windows or in the backs of other cars. Make use of your ears; it is possible to detect the direction of approach (right or left) of a vehicle coming from behind, and whether it is accelerating or slowing. Don't muffle these valuable detectors with hoods or personal stereos.

On narrow roads with parked cars or other obstructions remember that the convention is that traffic on the same side as the obstruction gives way to traffic coming in the opposite direction.

If somebody else does you a favour—waves you on, stops to leave a gap for you to turn right across a line of slow-moving cars or whatever—give them a wave and a smile. Whether you like it or not, all the time you are on a bicycle (and come to that, driving a car with bikes on a roof rack) you represent cycling and cyclists to the outside world. Since you're automatically an ambassador, be a diplomat too.

Don't try to compete in traffic with other cyclists—they may be more experienced, naturally faster or a great deal more foolhardy than you are.

Finally the most difficult rule of all: concentrate exclusively on the task in hand, clear everything else from your mind. In the country one of the great joys of cycling is just rolling along with your mind in neutral; in town it could be deadly.

Fig. 75 You may find it an advantage to incorporate bits of 'official' cycle route into your journey. These cyclists' traffic lights at the east end of London's Strand allow cyclists to go straight across from Wellington Street to Waterloo Bridge; other traffic has to make a 600 metre detour round the Aldwych.

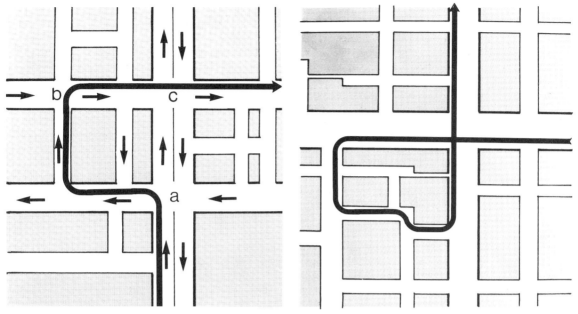

Fig. 73 The official manoeuvre for turning right from London's Marylebone Road, a dual carriageway, onto Gloucester Place, the A41 and one of the main ways out northwards. The right turns are made easy by using one-way streets; there are also sequenced traffic lights at *a*, *b* and *c*. The direct right turn at *c*—which would be impracticable for a cyclist anyway—is not permitted

Fig. 74 A comparable manoeuvre that you might devise at a hypothetical junction to avoid being stuck in the middle between streams of fast-moving traffic. In general the left-left-left sequence is more easily followed than the left-right-right at the Marylebone Road-Gloucester Place intersection in the other diagram

Designing an urban route

Obviously it is more pleasant to ride as far as possible on roads which are quiet and carry little traffic. It may be feasible to link apparently dead-end roads with short sections of cyclable path.

Inevitably, however, you will encounter busier roads at times. The main concern is to devise a route which will make it easier to join, cross and leave such roads in safety.

Cross or join busy roads at traffic lights where at all possible, for the best chance of joining the traffic flow. If you can, leave such a road by a left turn. As far as possible ensure that right turns off this type of road are at junctions with lights and/or protective bollards. Almost anything is better than being stranded out there with fast traffic in either direction on both sides of you. In a number of cases there are 'official' loops or it is quite possible to devise similar loops of your own.

Avoid fast busy roads where a motorway or trunk road debouches onto city streets—particularly those with fast slip roads leaving or joining. These involve you in crossing obliquely streams of fast-moving traffic. And of course avoid this type of surburban trunk road itself. Also avoid as far as you can large fast roundabouts—unless they are controlled by lights. (Hyde Park Corner roundabout in London, for example, is quite easily negotiated by cyclists now that entry to it is controlled by traffic lights. Before, it was almost impossible.)

Learn which are the useful one-way streets where you filter across with the traffic to make your exit from the road easy. Learn the directions in which most of the traffic habitually travels. That way you'll know whether to be in the lanes which are part of that stream, if you want to go the same way, or in a definitely different lane if you don't. Learn the timing sequence of traffic light changes; it's useful to know when it's worth hurrying and when it's not. There's no point in a spirited sprint to be first to a red light.

If there are signposted cycle routes it may well be advantageous to incorporate them or parts of them. Often lights sequences will have been adjusted to help cyclists through or small sections of a cycle-only route may have been introduced to avoid congested junctions or danger spots.

SIXTEEN

MAPS AND USING THEM

A map holds the key to unknown country, shows how to get to the places you want to visit and how to avoid the ones you don't. The best ones can reveal the very nature of the terrain you'll be in and often give some idea of its formation and human history.

Maps for the cyclist

The traditional cyclist's maps were always the Ordnance Survey's one-inch-to-the-mile and John Bartholomew's half-inch-to-the-mile series. These are now mostly superseded by the metric 1:50000 and 1:100000 scales respectively. Ordnance Survey maps at the 1:250000 (about four miles to the inch, or 2.5km to the cm) and the 1:25000 (about 2½in to the mile, or 4cm to the km) scales also have their uses.

Ordnance Survey 1:50000 'Landranger' series

The country is covered by 204 sheets, each showing an area 40 × 40km (about 25 miles square). The Landranger series with its lurid magenta covers has superseded the interim First Series, which was a photographic enlargement of the last of the inch-to-the-mile editions. Clarity is claimed to be increased, although the uniform weight of the Teutonic typeface lacks the variety and typographical elegance of the older maps. This scale is the most generally useful to the cycle-tourist: it is the smallest scale to show every metalled road and every topographical feature of note. These maps also show rights of way in England and Wales.

As far as route following goes, these maps are superb. However they do have disadvantages. The method of indicating relief—hills and valleys—although detailed, is by contour lines and spot heights, which offer a less immediate appreciation of the terrain than layer tints (usually green at low levels grading to brown at higher) used on some other maps. Hills and valleys are important news for the bicyclist. The unfolding of the sheets demands topological impossibilities of the paper at the corners of the folds and

would appear to have been designed by someone who has never had to open up a map in any sort of breeze. The folded size is slightly large for the pocket (about 23 × 13cm) and the map has almost to be screwed up to fit into any map holder or map pocket. But I would feel lost travelling in Britain without a map of this detail and quality. Ideally, when unfolded, a map should show a square area; the standard Landranger unfold gives you about 20 × 11km. (The French Michelin maps have the right idea: a single unfold gives two tall thin panels side-by-side to make up a square.)

The art of practical map reading lies in relating the country you are in to its representation on the map. Many features are depicted by conventional signs—churches, buildings of all sorts, windmills, radio masts, railways, water features and so on: there is no short cut, they have to be learned from the key down the right-hand side of the map. The colour conventions for roads are becoming universal: blue for motorways, red for main A-class roads, orangey-brown for B-class secondary roads, yellow for most other tarred roads, at least in the country, and uncoloured for unmetalled tracks or other roads and drives in towns.

It is by the yellow roads that you will generally be travelling, or some of the less busy B-roads—and only infrequently on A-roads, when it cannot be avoided. The map distinguishes between 'Trunk' roads (with the suffix '(T)' after the road number on the map), which are likely to carry the heaviest traffic, and other, lesser, main roads. Traffic density will also vary with time of day, day of the week, time of the year and area of the country. The A82(T) trunk road through Glencoe in the Scottish Highlands, quite busy in summer, carries in the autumn far less traffic than many minor roads in the Home Counties do all the year round. Some main roads with a nearby parallel motorway are relatively quiet.

Interpreting 'white' (uncoloured) roads on the map needs caution. They can vary from easily ridable—slightly rough or even slightly tarred and metalled—to near quagmires, varying with season, recent weather, usage by tractors or horses, locality and geology. The

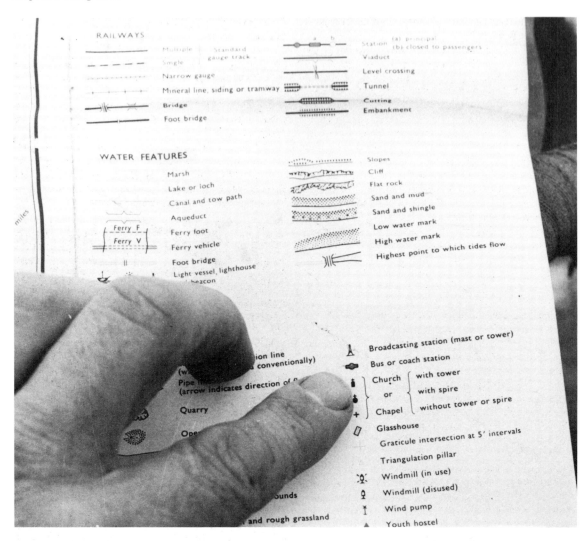

Fig. 76 The explanation of the symbols used on the Ordnance Survey 1:50000 map is given down the right-hand side of each sheet.

main clue from the map as to the passability of a white road is its apparent purpose. If it links two settlements, hamlets say, and is not too long then it is likely that it is used to travel from one to the other and is probably easily passable. If there are houses along it, then it is obviously used for access. If it seems to link nowhere with nowhere, then expect it to be more agricultural; if there's a house or farm close to one end, then that end is probably used for access and in fair condition—the rest may not be.

Whether or not a white road on the map is a right of way is not easy to resolve. If it is shown as a 'byway open to all traffic' (alternate red crosses and dots) or as

a bridleway (red dashes) as well there is no question. The status of 'roads used as public paths' ('RUPP's—alternating red dots and dashes) is vague: these RUPPs are being progressively reclassified as byways, bridle-ways or footpaths. It would seem unlikely that there would be any objection to cyclists using remaining RUPPs. Rights of way may be obscure on the ground: a right of way is no guarantee of a practical, even less ridable, route. If a map shows a white road coming to a stop and continuing as a marked right of way the implication is that the public has a right of way to reach the start of the path. However, beware—right-of-way information is prepared from definitive maps held by the local authority and such information may not be available for the whole of a particular Ordnance Survey sheet. A small pink square part way down the legend at the right of the map shows the extent of right-of-way information.

Of more than passing interest to the cyclist is the marking of steep hills. Very steep hills—on yellow or higher graded roads only—are indicated by chevrons across the road; perversely, these point *downhill*. Two chevrons close together mark a hill steeper than 20 per cent (1-in-5 or about 11 degrees, fairly steep); one-chevron hills are between 20 per cent and 14 per cent (1-in-5 and 1-in-7, about 8-11 degrees). For the record, there is a patch of land about 5km by 3km, east of the Conwy Valley in North Wales, near the village of Eglwysbach, with no less than 14 sets of single chevrons and six sets of double ones. This is in the allegedly non-mountainous part of North Wales. You may find it less dispiriting to go up a relatively short steep hill and down a long gradual one rather than the other way round. A useful rule of thumb is to add an hour to the day's expected journey time (or knock off an hour's worth of miles) for each 300m (1000ft) of actual climb.

The map shows 'fenced' and 'unfenced' roads: the side or sides that have no enclosure are dashed. In open country an unfenced road may mean easy access to moorland or common land for, say, a picnic meal; it may also mean that views are unobscured. A 'fenced' road is just as likely, in many places, to be hedged or walled and may be more sheltered on a windy day. Roads through woodland (wooded areas are marked in green) are likely to be more sheltered, as are winding roads through valleys. Unfenced roads across flat countryside and roads along the tops or ridges of hills are likely to be exposed. In very flat country, such as the Fens, a fence is likely to be no more than a strand or two of wire, and the road to be above the level of the fields; given the wrong day some Fenland roads are harder than mountain passes.

Common to all Ordnance Survey maps is the system of co-ordinates for giving the position of an object, known as the National Grid. Maps of a scale of one-inch-to-a-mile and larger are divided into kilometre squares and the legend at the side of the map shows how to quote the 'Grid Reference' of the 100m square within which a given point lies. The 10km squares of the 1:250000 map allow the specification of a 1km square. Many organisations—such as accommodation and tourist guide compilers, even signposts in Dorset—give positions by means of these grid references.

Finally the Landranger series shows a variety of what the Survey terms 'tourist information', including the position of picnic-sites, camp-sites, beauty-spots, youth-hostels, information centres—and public conveniences in rural areas.

Ordnance Survey 'One-inch' 1:63360 'Tourist' maps

The old order lives on in the shape of nine special 'tourist' sheets, covering popular scenic areas. Some have layer tints and hill shading to show relief. The sheets available are Ben Nevis and Glencoe, Loch Lomond and the Trossachs (these Scottish ones are extremely attractive maps), Lake District, North York Moors, Peak District, Cotswold, New Forest, Exmoor and, finally, Dartmoor. A tenth sheet at the half-inch (1:126720) scale covers Snowdonia and Anglesey, while an eleventh at 1:50000 covers the Norfolk Broads, more from the point of view of the water-borne than the landlubber.

Fig. 77 The neat and essentially simple Maptrap by CJ Designs

Bartholomew's 1:100000 National map

'Barts' Half-Inch, the cyclist's old favourite—at its colourful best the most visually attractive map produced of the British Isles—has been replaced by the slightly larger scale 1:100000 'National' series. This is a partially revised photographic enlargement from the original 1:126720. Rather oddly the detail shown has been slightly reduced. The map now shows rather a clash of typefaces between the attractive hand-lettering of the original and the later mechanically-produced type. However, with the provisos which applied to the os Landranger, it remains a reasonably practical map for the cyclist. You have to be even more careful in interpreting a 'white' road on 'Barts'. 'Wide' white roads are nearly always fine; 'narrow' white roads may range from firm or even metalled roads down to scarcely visible traces. The fold, is like the os Landranger with the same drawbacks and a slightly-larger-than-pocketable closed size. The opened size, 27×37cm ($10\frac{1}{2} \times 14\frac{1}{2}$in) is more manageable than the os, and at the smaller scale covers a useful 26×33km of terrain. Experience with foreign maps, particularly French and Swiss, suggest that a good 1:100000 map would be close to the cyclist's ideal scale.

One other Bartholomew product which can be unreservedly recommended for tour planning is their annually revised 1:300000 atlas. With clear layer shading and a logical continuity from page to page it is very easy to read and shows detail comparable with the os 1:250000 atlas (below). Atlases are not appropriate for carrying on the bicycle but are excellent for planning.

Ordnance Survey 1:250000 or 'Quarter-inch' 'Routemaster'

This map covers the country in only nine sheets. It can be useful for the cyclist for route planning or even for use on the road for relatively direct journeys. Only classified M, A and B class roads are coloured. Not quite all other roads are shown, confusing where a marked corner turns out to be a junction, but you can take it that all those shown are cyclable. The map gives a fair impression of relief by layer tints in various shades of brown. Rights of way and other detailed information are not given, but some 'tourist information'—including a selection of camp sites—is shown.

For route planning this map, too, is available in atlas form—in what must be one of the most awkward designs ever as far as page-to-page continuity goes. The atlas includes a complete gazeteer-index of marked place-names.

Ordnance Survey 1:25000 'Pathfinder' series

This is a very much more detailed map than the 1:50000. The original First Series, each sheet covering a 10km square, has been largely replaced by the new-style Pathfinder sheets, most of which cover 20km west-to-east by 10km south-to-north. The newer map also employs a wider range of colours. Detail down to field boundaries and small ponds is shown, and such features as farms with outbuildings are indicated with

their approximate on-the-ground shape and scale. The Pathfinder sheets in England and Wales also show rights of way and some 'tourist information'. The updating rate has been accelerated over the last few years.

The same map is also used as the base for the Outdoor Leisure series, 27 sheets, covering rather larger areas than the Pathfinder ones. Localities include the Cairngorms, the Cuillins with Torridon, the Three Peaks, the Lake District, Malham and Upper Wharfedale, North York Moors, Peak District, Snowdonia National Park, Brecon Beacons National Park, Wye Valley and Forest of Dean, and several smaller areas in southern England. Designed principally for walkers, these sheets show such items as camp sites, mountain and cave rescue posts, land to which the public has access, and access paths, as well as the detail of the base map—all very useful for cycling off the beaten track.

Lost

Everybody gets a little unsure where they are from time to time. If you remember passing a road junction a short way back, retrace; if not, stop or go gently on to the next. If, however, the road ahead goes steeply downhill, say off the ridge of a hill, it is obviously prudent to try to keep what height you have and to stop immediately and look for clues. You should know where you are within a mile or two, so you will not have to search too great an area.

First, are there any signposts which will suggest where you might be? Does the direction of the roads conform with the map? Are you at a prominent bend in the road? On top or at the foot of a hill? Is there a large farm or house nearby which might be named on the map? Are there any topographical features—valleys, streams, woods, orchards, quarries, end of an unfenced stretch of road—which fit in (caution: it is quite easy for an unfenced road to have become fenced since the map was made or, particularly in the agribusiness prairies of East Anglia, the reverse)? Are there any man-made features—railway bridges, level crossings, churches (with or without towers or spires), pubs, windmills, windpumps, overhead power lines, isolated telephone boxes, signposted footpaths or bridleways leaving the road, milestones, canals?

In a town or village, is there a street name which suggests which road you are on, for example 'Birmingham Road'. Telephone boxes and letter boxes usually indicate where they are, so do railway stations and hospitals. Finally, you can sink your pride and ask—in fact, if you open a map within a hundred yards of a non-cyclist they'll come and ask whether you are lost!

Even the old dodges for determining the compass directions are worth remembering: the sun actually *is* somewhere towards the south at midday (or 1p.m. British Summer Time) and moves round from east to west at half the speed of the clock; lichen and moss really do grow more readily on the shaded, north side of trees, posts, walls and buildings; churches lie roughly on a west-east line, some with great accuracy; at night the 'Pointers' of the Plough point to the Pole Star, which is very close to due north.

SEVENTEEN

STOPPING PLACES

Food and drink

Obtaining food on the road is easier now that more pubs are providing food, ranging from bar snacks and sandwiches to quite elaborate meals. Many also have an area which is set aside principally for the service of food and to which children under 14 may legally be admitted. Some breweries issue lists of pubs offering food. Local tourist information offices can provide these, as well as lists of cafés and restaurants. Several cycling clubs and organisations publish lists from time to time and these are usually noted in the cycling press. The Little Chef and Happy Eater franchise chains of café/restaurants supply maps showing where their various establishments are. Many are quite well out in the country although, by their nature, beside main roads.

There are fewer opportunities on Sundays and it is worth noting some of the other possibilities of at least a cup of tea. Most 'garden centres' and 'craft centres' seem to include a small cafeteria as do the larger National Trust properties and other houses or gardens open to the public. Many railway and bus stations have cafeterias or refreshment rooms; the rail ones are listed in the British Rail timetable. Rather unpredictably, such organisations as Women's Institutes and church fabric fund-raisers run coffee and tea stalls at village halls and churches.

Pubs and even cafes tend to be shut just at that mid-afternoon time when your drinking bottle needs replenishing. Roadside taps have diminished in number of recent years, although some remain. Building sites will almost always have a tap, and most churchyards. Some railway stations have drinking water, but not many. Most ordinary householders, asked politely, will be quite happy to fill a bottle or two.

Overnight accommodation

Where you stop depends entirely on inclination and your means. The cheapest is with relatives or friends;

many youthful first tours have been dictated by the location of strategically-placed aunts and second cousins. Next (apart from kitting yourself out) comes camping which has a chapter following this one all to itself.

Many, particularly young, cyclists' introduction to cycle-touring has been by way of youth hostels. There are about 250 in England and Wales and some 80 in Scotland; addresses of the organisations and more details are given in Appendix 1. The coverage is generally good although recent tendencies to polarise the YHA, particularly, into large hostels suitable for groups and fewer small and remote ones for enthusiasts has left gaps in places. A few private establishments are run on similar lines, such as the Camping Barns administered by the Peak Park Planning Board and the halts of the Gatliffe Trust. Hostel accommodation is mainly in single-sex dormitories, some large, some small, and members are required to carry out simple jobs connected with the running and maintenance of the hostel during their stay. Blankets or duvets are provided on the bunk-type beds; members must supply or hire a sheet sleeping bag. Prices vary with the member's age and the hostel's amenities. Most provide fairly simple meals; almost all have kitchens for members' use. Hostels occupy a range of buildings from National Trust-owned castles to converted hunting lodges and remote farm cottages. At many, advance booking is desirable at popular holiday weekends and in late July and August; Bank Holiday dates differ in England and Wales and Scotland, while there are also local holidays and holiday weeks in Scotland. Many hostels are closed for quite extended periods in late autumn, winter and early spring.

The traditional halts for touring cyclists were, and often still are, 'Bed and Breakfast' houses. These are private homes whose owners let a room or two to passing travellers, often at prices competitive with youth hostels. Local tourist offices and regional tourist boards publish lists. The same authorities also list guest houses, small private hotels and of course the larger ones. Most accommodation, apart from hostels,

Fig. 78 Food and drink are never very far from the cycle-tourist's thoughts

is organised on a couple basis and is easier to find, or a good deal less expensive, for two people than one.

Cycling 'centre-tours' from one or more fixed centres can be very enjoyable. Self-catering holidays at rented cottages or flats are increasingly popular and lend themselves well to this type of cycling. The best type of centre offers several routes out, with a variety of terrain, and is inland; a seaside location immediately halves the directions available. You could well divide a fortnight's holiday between two or even more centres. 'Centre-touring' lends itself particularly well to families or to outings by riders of mixed ability; little baggage has to be carried, different length routes can be planned, while members of the party need not all do the same thing on any given day.

EIGHTEEN

CYCLE CAMPING

Cycling camping offers at its best the ultimate in freedom, but means acquiring a lot of extra equipment—and being prepared to carry it. This means low gears, acceptance of a sometimes restricted mileage and a different feel to the bicycle.

Tents

If you know it's going to be a fine night you can sleep under the stars with only a groundsheet or a bivvy bag. But for most of us, camping means a tent. For British Isles camping it is desirable to have a double-skinned type, with an impermeable outer tent coming right down to the ground all round and a breathable inner with sewn-in groundsheet. Given British weather it is also desirable that the outer can be put up first.

A reasonable definition of 'lightweight' for a tent is up to around 1.8kg (4lb) for a one-person tent and 3.2kg (7lb) for two. They can be variants of the traditional ridge tent or newer 'hooped' or 'dome' designs.

Outer tents are made of a proofed nylon fabric, impermeable to rain and impermeable to moisture from the inside, so that condensation builds up. The inner tent is made of a porous 'breathable' material, cotton, polyester or uncoated nylon or a mixture. The separation between the two prevents condensation damping the inner tent and also confers some heat insulation. A substantial, sewn-in groundsheet, preferably in a slight tray shape with 8–10cm walls, is essential. A heavier gauge groundsheet can be a desirable feature. There is an immense range of lightweight tents on the market and it pays to look around, and to shop around. Check how small a package the poles or hoops make when dismantled; packages longer than about 45–50cm are difficult to accommodate on a bicycle. If you are buying a two-person tent for two people to share check how the load is divisible between two if necessary. A good lightweight tent is not cheap; typical prices run out at about two-thirds the cost of a handbuilt cycle frame.

Sleeping bags

Sleeping bags are graded according to the number of 'seasons' they are adjudged suitable for. The grades go up to five: the fifth 'season' is mountain use in winter and is warm in temperatures down to about $-35°C$. A three- or four-season bag ($-5°C$ and $-20°C$ respectively) is adequate for most cycling use. Fillings are nowadays either natural down or down with increasing admixtures of small feathers, billed as 'down/feather' or 'feather/down' according to the preponderant species, or synthetic fillings such as Du Pont Hollofil. Down bags are lighter and pack smaller for a given performance but lose insulation if they get wet. Polyester fillings retain much of their effectiveness even if damp and are easier to clean. Synthetic filled bags are about a third to a half the price of comparable down ones. In our unit of currency a good down bag costs as much as a handbuilt bicycle frame, a top-quality five-season one up to twice as much. A down bag will fit in quite a small front pannier; a synthetic one requires a medium sized one. Bags should be stuffed into their containers; it's worth while lining the pannier with a polyethylene bag. (One of the many First Rules of Camping is: 'There is no such thing as too many plastic bags'.) It is essential that your sleeping bag should be kept dry. Bags should be liberated from the compression of carrying as soon as possible to allow them to regain their 'loft'.

Insulating mats

One of the greatest additions to lightweight camping comfort of the last decade or two has been the introduction of closed-cell foam insulating mats—the yellow rolls that you see backpackers carrying. In use they are placed under the sleeping bag, not to make a soft bed (which they don't, particularly) but to insulate you from losing heat to the ground. They also keep you clear of any moisture which might condense or collect on the groundsheet. Although bulky they are very light and can easily be rolled up and strapped to the top of the rear carrier. The best known is the yellow Karrimat by Karrimor, available in a variety of lengths and widths.

Cooking

What you need for cooking while camping depends entirely on your intentions. The basic necessities are some form of stove—open fires are not practical, and often not permitted, in many places—and some pots and pans.

Small gas stoves are powered by liquefied petroleum gas, usually butane, with or without a proportion of propane. The portable versions such as the Tilley models or Camping Gaz s200 are the handiest for camping because of their ease of starting and control. Heat output is, however, limited and they need shelter in all but a dead calm. Performance tends to fall off

from about 5°C downwards, giving a poor flame but a dash of propane helps no end. A palliative on a cold morning is to pop the (unlit) stove in your sleeping bag for half an hour before you get up. These are the cleanest stoves to carry but the most expensive to run although cheap to buy.

Small '½ pint' paraffin pressure stoves—the archetypal Primus or Optimus, both from Sweden—give out a good deal more heat but are slower to start; they also require a second fuel, usually methylated spirit, to 'prime' them for starting. The worst snag is that they require the carriage of paraffin (kerosene). Once this fuel escapes the smell (and real or imagined taste on everything within reach) is very difficult to eradicate. The fuel is best carried outside the bicycle in a metal bottle in a bottle cage, while the stove itself is best carried either completely separately on a frame-fitting clip or sealed up in a side-pocket used for nothing else. The stoves are quite expensive initially but are very cheap to run.

Petrol stoves are easier to start, give out more heat but share high initial cost and a smelly liquid fuel. They are designed to run on unleaded petrol (otherwise they eventually clog up), which usually means buying special fuel.

Methylated spirit stoves are intermediate in heat output but rather bulky. They are easy to start and cheap to run, and meths evaporates quite quickly if spilt.

The most practical pans are the spun aluminium type marketed in Britain under the brand-name Bulldog, or similar versions, sold in sets of three or more. It is often possible to pack other items inside these pans in the panniers; you can almost persuade yourself that they don't take up any room. You will also need a plate (a plastic one about 20cm in diameter), a cup or mug (plastic practical, enamelled steel doesn't taste but gets hot) and cutlery—a perfectly ordinary set of stainless knife, fork and two spoons is best. A very useful addition is a sharp serrated steel knife such as a 10cm Kitchen Devil. You will also need a can opener, bottle opener and corkscrew to become a truly sybaritic cycle-camper.

It is almost impossible to synchronise dishes in camp cooking or to keep them hot. Develop a taste for 'serial' meals, where you have items one after the other rather than together, or 'one-pot' meals, such as stews. Avoid frying—degreasing the pans before packing them away is often difficult.

Fig. 79 The small gas stove is quite cheap to buy, easy to start and clean to use and carry but has limited power and is relatively expensive to run

Fig. 80 It was a wet windy evening when we pitched camp, so we chose a well-drained spot with the tent pointing down the slight slope and made the most of the shelter of the trees. The tent is a Vango Force Ten 2CN with home-made bell-end extension

Sites and pitching

Official sites are useful for such facilities as hot water, laundering or a small store. Many farms will accept a small tent or two for one night. In wild country where the land is not in obvious agricultural use there is usually no objection to a single-night stop. It should go without saying that you will neither leave litter nor pollute streams or lakes. If possible, check with somebody nearby.

The ideal pitching spot is quiet, level, well-drained and sheltered, and high enough above any stream for it not to encroach if it rises rapidly, as streams can in mountain areas. Failing a level patch, align the tent so that your feet are downhill but the tent is level crossways. The back end of the tent should be towards the wind, leaving the front sheltered as far as possible. If possible avoid pitching directly under trees, particularly in high winds, heavy rain or during the season when they drop sticky buds on you—but make use of the 'wind shadow' of trees. Try out your beautiful new equipment near home before embarking into the unknown.

Keeping warm

It's easy to stay snug and smug in bed as the rain lashes down inches away from your nose—a strangely cheering experience. A small double-skinned tent soon warms up inside but the Great World Outside doesn't. Change your top-half of clothing as soon as you pitch camp; the slight residual dampness from sweating can soon chill you. A Helly-Hansen Lifa vest is very comforting plus a layer more than you expected to need on top. If you do get chilled get into your sleeping bag fully clothed until you get warm. (Although generally the warmest and most comfortable clothing for actually sleeping in a bag is as little as possible.) Order your chores to enable them to be done from inside the tent, by arranging all you need to hand. For breakfast have the requisites—including water—placed so that you do not need to leave your sleeping bag to cook and consume your meal. Whenever you are cooking in the tent porch, peg stoves down to avoid any chance of upsetting them.

Avoid letting the tent inner get wetter than necessary. You can pack the tent outer away when wet, segregated from dry things, but take the inner down inside first. Nylon outer tents can stand being wet for a day or two; cotton inners cannot. Keep them well aired.

Fig. 81 For camping the second bottle cage is very useful, either for water or liquid fuel. This position leaves the seat tube free for a frame-fitting pump

Camping and the bicycle

Camping equipment makes a rather heavier and bulkier load than you may be used to. Low gears are definitely needed and 60–80km/day (35–50 miles) is plenty. Stout and rigid carriers are essential and the load is best divided between front and rear panniers. Pack the bulky things, most spare clothes, stoves, cooking pots, part of the tent—things not wanted on the road—in the rear panniers. The Karrimat, maybe part or all of the tent, and sundries such as cameras and waterproofs, may be strapped across the carrier. Into the front panniers go on one side the sleeping bag and on the other various items that *are* likely to be wanted on the voyage such as extra pullovers, gloves, yet more cameras, lenses and film, maps and money. The heavier load makes acceleration slower; cultivate the habit of changing down before stopping. Steering and handling are also generally heavier. 'Honking' may well be impracticable.

To avoid having to strike camp every day it is a good plan to spend two or three nights at a suitable site and to travel out relatively unladen from there for a couple of days. Do not despise out-and-home journeys, particularly in mountain areas. We have spent some

very enjoyable spells in the Alps, travelling up a different valley each day. You enjoy on the way back the views that you didn't turn round to see on the way out, and if you make the more strenuous part of your journey in the morning while you are fresh and it is cooler, the return is easier when you are weary.

NINETEEN

OFF THE BEATEN TRACK

There are whole organisations devoted to cycling away from metalled roads: the Rough-Stuff Fellowship, which might be described as the conventional-bicycle wing, and the newer National Off-Road Bicycle Association, which devotes itself to mountain-bikes. Members of both sometimes carry out hair-raising feats to cross uncharted wastes; I am more timid. For me a rough path or track has to be essentially ridable, for at least a major part of its length, and it has to lead to or pass through somewhere worth the effort.

Many of the features of the mountain-bike make good sense for off-road riding, particularly low gears, fatter tyres and good clearances between wheels and frame. On a more conventional bicycle 35 or 40mm tyres, inflated to a moderate 3 bar or so (45–50psi) are certainly preferable to narrow, highly inflated ones. Wheels should be robust. Take care that nothing fragile in your bag can be damaged by vibration or bouncing.

Follow the same guidelines as anyone else in wild, and particularly high, country. Have enough clothing (even an easily-carried survival bag) and high-energy reserve food for emergency; make sure somebody knows where you are going, by what route, and when you expect to return or to reach your new destination; think at least twice before making a wild crossing alone. Be prudent: minor accidents, trivial or laughed off a couple of miles from home, could be a disaster 15 miles from civilisation on a mountain track in deteriorating weather. Weather can change fast in the hills. Don't be too proud to turn back, and if it gets worse suddenly take the fastest practicable route to low ground. If you change your plans make sure that those who might otherwise raise the alarm know that you are safe.

Never overestimate your ability in this sort of country. Even on roads daily mileages are low in tough country and even less on unmetalled tracks. For example a mainly ridable track in central Wales, and one which doesn't pass over particularly high ground (the one from the Caban Côch reservoir in the Elan Valley by way of the shore of the Claerwen reservoir to

Ffair Rhos), took a group of six experienced riders about four and a half hours for the 16km (10 miles) from metalled road to metalled road. This included an hour's picnic lunch stop, a factor you should include in our calculations.

Fords fascinate many cycle-tourists, but treat them with care. Fords on metalled roads are usually ridable (there's often a footbridge) but some can be impressively slimy and slippery. Follow a straight line as far as you can, use a low gear and if possible reconnoitre the shallowest, smoothest and firmest line. Vulnerable pedal bearings are only about 10cm (4in) from the ground at their lowest point, and the expensive bottom bracket only a little over 25cm (10in). If you *do* get water in them, lay the bicycle on its side to drain and regrease them at the earliest opportunity. Or you can wade through and if need be carry the bicycle.

When wheeling or riding a bicycle over any rocky section take care to avoid hitting vulnerable parts, particularly gear mechanism, cranks, pedals or outer chainring, against rocks or stones.

With low gears a surprising amount is ridable, often more easily than walking. Always keep one eye open for a dry spot to put your foot down if you are forced to a stop. Some rock surfaces—chalk is the worst—can become unbelievably slippery when wet.

Use the techniques for easing your weight off the saddle to smooth your path on rocky stretches. On steep descents you will need to keep your weight well back and to brake with care. If you're in doubt about staying in command, get off; an unridable buckled wheel, or worse an unwheelable one, could be more than a fleeting nuisance.

You will of course need good maps—at least 1:50000, often 1:25000—and to be able to use them. Navigation will often be by the shape of features such as ridges and the position of stream valleys and re-entrant contours or stone walls. There are few signposts in such places. A compass is also useful if visibility worsens.

Don't let this talk of hazards and precautions put you off; the best upland tracks offer the ultimate in

Fig. 82 Negotiating a shallow watersplash on Cannock
Chase. Deeper ones call for more care

cycle-touring experiences. The Roman road over the Brecon Beacons, several of the crossings of the Black Mountains in Powys, the Salter Fell road across Bowland in Lancashire and many more offer amazing vistas and a sense of solitude and of being on top of the world that rivals even the high passes of the Alps.

TWENTY

CYCLING OUT OF SEASON

There are rewards in cycle-touring in the winter, and the late autumn and early spring months either side. Traffic is generally lighter and places which are overrun in summer revert to a pleasing tranquillity: this is probably the best season for seeing the West Country and the Lake District, for example. The end of autumn is a colourful time almost everywhere and in mountain country there is a fleeting season—late October to the end of November—where it is golden autumn in the valleys and already snowy winter on the tops. In late February and March signs of spring appear at low levels while snow still dwells on the summits. You can choose your season by how high you climb. And there is at times a pleasing openness to the leafless vistas.

Fig. 83 The fewer delicate components you expose to the rigours of winter, the better

The winter bicycle

The bicycle is already a fairly simple mechanism and one of the best ways of preparing it for the winter is to simplify it even further. Salt from treated roads or the thin slime of mud at other times is the enemy of chains, bearings and gear mechanisms. It is well worth having a less lavishly equipped bicycle for winter.

I would strongly advocate using a single gear in winter. For one thing, a single gear offers fewer pieces of delicate mechanism to be sacrificed to the winter elements. Second, the discipline of a single gear, by making you pedal a little faster than you might choose at times, and at others making you push, inculcates a degree of both suppleness and strength. A fixed gear, without freewheel, gives you a feeling of oneness with the machine, leading to a greater measure of fine control of speed and braking.

Wheels for single-gear use are usually built without 'dishing'—symmetrically above the hub flanges—and have threadings both sides. For fixed gear use there are two threadings, about a 5–6mm width of right-hand thread at normal diameter and pitch (1.37in × 24TPI) and a 3–4mm of smaller diameter *left-hand* thread for a lockring to prevent the sprocket coming unscrewed when you brake by easing back on the pedals. You can at a pinch use a fixed sprocket on an ordinary freewheel threading, retaining it by a bottom bracket lockring. Done up tight, this should be proof against all normal back pedalling. It is not usually possible to use directly a dished wheel for a single gear except with a single sprocket on a multiple freewheel body; the threading is too far from the rear fork end.

Ensure that the chainring and rear sprocket are in line to within about 3mm by juggling bottom bracket axle lengths and packing washers for the rear hub. Use a straight edge to check.

Your are unlikely to find $\frac{1}{2} \times \frac{3}{32}$in derailleur-chain-fitting single freewheels nowadays in sizes other than 16 or 18T; you could use the wider $\frac{1}{2} \times \frac{1}{8}$in (12.7 × 3.18mm) chain for which larger freewheels *are* available, a single $\frac{1}{2} \times \frac{3}{32}$in sprocket screwed onto a

Fig. 84 The fixed sprocket on its hub with the lighter-toned lockring to prevent its unscrewing under reverse thrust. The chain tension is adjusted by moving the wheel forward or backwards in the slot. A quick-release rear hub is only to be recommended for fixed wheel use for light or gentle riders

multiple freewheel body such as a Regina, or a splined sprocket on a Sun Tour or similar body with another, threaded, sprocket as a retaining ring. A suitable gear, to start with, is in the range 60–65in. Single freewheels usually have 16 to 20 teeth, so you need a chainring between about 40 and 47 with 18, 19 or 20-tooth freewheels. Fixed sprockets are available up to 22 teeth, giving a wider choice of chainring size, and in the $\frac{3}{32}$in width.

The chain is tensioned by moving the wheel forwards or backwards in the rear fork end slots. When properly adjusted it should not be possible to move the chain up or down more than about 15mm at its slackest point, halfway between the bottom of the sprocket and chainwheel. Solid-axle rear hubs with 'track-nut' fixing are generally best for fixed-wheel use.

A fixed gear needs a bit of practice before you stop trying to freewheel round corners or to flip the cranks backwards to the right position for starting off. You will soon learn to lift the back of the bicycle just off the ground to bring the pedals back to the right point for starting. The perpetual motion is less of a hardship than it might seem except in viciously hilly country, and helps to keep you warm in the cold. Obviously the fixed wheel isn't the thing for a mountain tour, nor for camping. But it's a fine tool for winter riding in gentler country, even if you never get to the point of relishing it purely for the pleasure of riding downhill and pedalling—as between-the-wars cycle-touring evangelist 'Wayfarer' put it—'like three men and a boy'.

In winter make sure that wheel, pedal and bottom bracket bearings are packed with clean, soft grease. Ensure that the front mudflap is doing its job.

Winter tyres need to be fairly substantial. Some local authorities panic at the first suggestion of frost and cover the road in salt 'n' gravel puncture mixture. Tyre tread pattern doesn't within reason seem to have much effect on roadholding, and some of the complicated ones can pick up and retain flints in what are, I understand, termed the sipes. A fairly plain rib or file

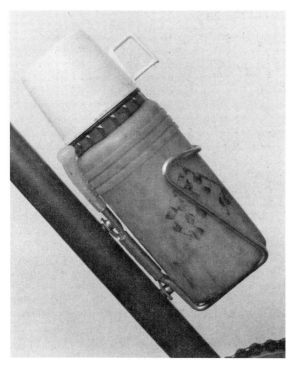

Fig. 85 A handy winter bottle—a small vacuum flask fitted into an old cut-down cycle bottle

pattern of adequate cross-section is as good as most; some knobbly tyres are rather hoppy on corners.

It is useful to be able to carry a hot drink or soup. Flasks in saddlebags or panniers can make quite a mess if they get broken and I prefer to carry a drink on the outside. Some small vacuum flasks—I've seen examples in Woolworths and other chain stores—are of a diameter to fit unmodified into bottle cages. An alternative is to fit a complete slim flask—or just the vacuum inner padded out with plastic foam—into an old cage-fitting drinking bottle with the top cut off.

Winter roads—and tracks

The main extra hazards on winter roads are snow and ice. Even quite modest changes of altitude can affect road conditions—you can quite often escape, if you want to, by dropping to lower ground. For example, one early November day in mid-Scotland it was a warm and sunny autumn morning after night frost at Aberfeldy (90m, 295ft up) at around 9a.m.; by 11a.m. we had reached patchy ice on the road at 200m (650ft); and by noon at Loch Kinarlochy at the 387m (1270ft) summit there was 5cm of snow on the road with the snow-capped 1083m cone of Schiehallion rearing up

above the forest. Even smaller differences between valleys and tops in such effete southern hills as the Chilterns or Cotswolds can have quite dramatic effects.

Clear skies and still air make for a wide range in daily temperatures with cold nights; cloud evens out night and day temperatures. Dull weather can, however, be a great deal more bleak and cold. On a sunny winter day with a clear sky it can begin freezing again about an hour before sunset, even at low levels. The lack of leaves on the trees, or of any trees at all, can make routes more exposed to the wind.

But there are compensations in the drama of the winter landscape which allows you to experience in Britain some of the brilliance of the snow-capped peaks we go to the Alps to seek in summer. A prolonged frosty spell can make some upland tracks much more pleasant, particularly some of the usually sloppier moorland ones. Certainly the best crossings we've made of—for example—Mastiles Lane in Yorkshire and of the Pont Scethin track in North Wales have been in February when they were frozen hard. And on a bright day in these conditions the surroundings can be breathtaking.

Don't let over-ambition spoil things. Work on the basis of a very modest speed, particularly through snow: you may have to walk stretches—even on a metalled road. And I mean *very* modest: say 2–3kph (1–1½mph) average, including stops, for a six-mile moorland crossing with 500m (1500ft) of climb in moderate (10cm) snow cover.

Riding on snow and ice calls for gentleness—in cornering, braking and acceleration—with rather less emphasis on the front brake than in the dry. If you see a frozen puddle or ice patch ride smoothly straight over it without braking or turning. Even if you're slowing down, momentarily stop braking as you cross it. This is where the gentle reverse thrust of the fixed wheel is a help.

Any part of the road with hoar frost crystals on it is much less slippery than bits which have been polished by traffic. Salted parts are less slippery—but still more than an ordinary wet road. You can detect the difference in tyre sound between a damp (unfrozen or salted) road and a frozen potentially icy one. On a rapidly cooling evening with damp roads the relative silence after the hiss of the wet can give early warning of freezing. As a damp road freezes the minuscule facets of the forming ice crystals give a myriad of scintillating reflections from the road surface which are quite distinctive, particularly by lamplight in the dark. Trees and buildings can inhibit freezing; take care when you come into the open again. On wet, muddy or icy roads it is helpful to use lower tyre pressures than in

119

the dry—ultimately down to perhaps 1½–2 bar (20–30psi) on ice.

Snow is different—an obstacle you have to plough through. Above a depth of 5–8cm it becomes noticeably hard work, reaching unridability when the pedals touch down at each revolution, at 10–12cm. But riding through 2–3cm of snow on a deserted road is strangely pleasant and almost eerily silent. In these conditions, tyres at normal pressures seem to cut through to the hard surface beneath. Tyres compress deeper snow and knobbly tyres then offer some advantage.

Not all snow is the same: in the languages of the Eskimos and Lapps there are 20 different words for snow. Soft powder snow, and any snow with small separate crystals at temperatures appreciably below freezing, is not particularly slippery. (What makes ice slippery is the micro-thin layer of water melted on its surface by the local pressure of the tyre on it.) Wetter snow is intrinsically more slippery and more readily compacted into a hard ice-like mass. Snow conditions change drastically as temperature rises and falls again through the day.

Snow builds up under mudguards and can clog the wheels if clearances are too tight. It also builds up round the brakes and can make their performance distinctly unimpressive. The normal warming-up of the rim when the blocks rub on it merely releases a thin slime of melting slush onto the braking surface. Stop and clear the build-up if serious braking is in prospect. In a dire emergency ride into a deeper patch of snow or onto a grass bank to stop.

Beaten-down snow is similar to ice but usually worn unevenly into ruts and ridges, and if refrozen after melting can be quite treacherous. Salted snow and slush rarely melt evenly and characteristics vary every few inches. The best way, which calls for a confidence you may not feel, is to relax and let the bike feel its own way a bit; don't grip the bars too hard. In the absence of other traffic it doesn't really matter if you fall off, particularly in snow. Check that there's nothing vulnerable in saddlebag side-pockets or panniers; the bicycle may just as easily slip over without you on it.

Modulate your effort as far as you can. Riding through snow can be very warm work but try to avoid becoming so damp through sweating that you risk chilling when you stop.

Night riding

The all-night ride, like winter riding, comes in the outside world's classification of abnormal behaviour. Quite a lot of cyclists might agree.

But a summer all-night ride—say in June or July when nights are relatively short—is an adventure not to be missed, at least once. The night brings a whole new range of sounds and smells, while to see the dawn breaking over upland country and to sense the world's reawakening, is to experience something that you will never forget.

It's surprising how cold it can get on a summer's night particularly under clear skies and just after dawn. You will need some of the trappings of winter cycling—gloves, hat, leg covering, an extra pullover or two—and something to eat at about the same hours as in daylight but 12 hours out of phase.

A vacuum flask or a small stove is useful. There is a very thin sprinkling of all-night cafes on main through routes, and the one or two motorway service areas accessible from other roads (such as Severn Bridge) are also open all night. Most of the Little Chef cafés open at seven—breakfast time.

However fast it may feel, night speed is about three-quarters daylight speed, so plan your distance accordingly. It helps to follow a simple route or one that you know, to cut down on map-reading. If you use dynamo lighting you'll need a small torch for the map; if you're using rechargeable batteries check that they'll last out. While many minor A-roads and B-roads are virtually deserted overnight, major commercial routes, and holiday ones (particularly towards the West Country) at the appropriate season, remain busy all the time. Sharing a fast main road with juggernauts at night is unwise.

Some people prefer to snatch a few minutes' sleep when they can, others prefer to stay awake all the time. Most have the odd drowsy bad patch and most ride out of them quite quickly. If you can't there's nothing for it but to stop and have a short sleep but keep warm.

By riding out overnight on Friday night and staying perhaps 120km (70 miles) from home on Saturday night you can avoid the anti-climactic effect of having to cover the last stages, weary and travel-worn, over familiar roads home. A 250km (150 mile) weekend gives you a chance of getting into some fresh country. You'll sleep for about ten hours on the Saturday night—and you'll have earned it.

TWENTY-ONE

GETTING THERE

You will probably need help at some time from public or private transport. Public transport is not really geared to carrying bicycles. If you have to travel at a given time or on a set day, such as when you are going on holiday, make it clear when booking that you want to take a bicycle.

Rail

Largely because of the departmental organisation of British Rail the rules for cycle carriage differ from region to region and between long-distance 'Inter-City' trains and suburban and local services. Further, the rules change with distressing frequency, as new types of rolling stock are introduced or transferred to different lines. British Rail produce explanatory leaflets.

At the time of writing there are no charges or restrictions for taking bicycles on many local services outside the London suburban area, nor on Inter-City services other than those operated by '125' High-Speed Trains. Because of the restricted space on 125s, carriage of bicycles is subject to a booking charge, reserving a place on a particular train. Larger parties may have further problems: the vans on 125s, cannot take more than five bicycles. Tandems, too, may encounter restrictions. On some local services, particularly those which have no guards or luggage compartments, cycles are banned, either altogether or during peak hours. On some suburban routes a flat-rate charge is made during peak hours. There appears to be no restriction on overnight and sleeper trains; check, though, that the train does not divide before your destination, and that the van will accompany you all the way.

Bicycles may not be taken on boat trains which carry passengers exclusively for cross-Channel boat services. On these, bicycles have to be registered as baggage to the Continental destination or the first Continental terminus. They may take some time to make the journey, since baggage usually goes on only one service per day. The well-heeled may note that bicycles are not carried on Pullman services either. They may be taken on the Gatwick Express service linking London Victoria with Gatwick Airport direct; these trains have spacious luggage vans and run very frequently, making Gatwick a convenient airport for cyclists.

Except where the bicycle travels as registered baggage, you have to place the bicycle in the guard's van yourself. It should be labelled with your name and destination—in theory one of the conditions of carriage. Make sure that the guard knows that you have a bicycle in the van and where you are going. Do not lock your bicycle to any fitting in the luggage van but do strap it with a toestrap or elastic strap so that it cannot fall. Don't leave it where it will obstruct a door—on either side of the train—nor where it blocks a corridor. Do not leave loose items or valuables on it.

Bicycles may be carried on London Transport lines which are operated by full-height trains and on the low 'tube' trains of the Central, Piccadilly, Bakerloo, Victoria and Jubilee lines where these run above ground. A half fare is payable and there are restrictions on time of use: not before 10a.m. nor during the evening peak period. There are no separate guards' compartments and you merely take the bicycle into the carriage with you.

Air travel

Bicycles may normally be taken on scheduled flights, either as part of the normal baggage allowance (15kg—about 33lb—on internal flights, 20kg (44lb) on European ones) or charged for as a separate piece of baggage, according to the airline. Over the free limit you may be asked to pay quite expensive excess baggage charges. Most modern aircraft require little dismantling of the machine, although it is always wise to remove the pedals. You will probably be asked to let the tyres down: a throwback to the days of unpressurised holds. You may occasionally have to take out the front wheel and mudguard (strapping them to the frame) and turn the handlebars in line with the top tube. Keep handy a small 25 × 25mm block of wood just over 100mm long to place between the fork ends to protect them. It is useful to pack a large piece of thick cardboard to cover the chain and gear mechanism. All loose fittings should be removed: bottles, pumps, bags, vulnerable parts of lamps, easily knocked out handle-bar end plugs. It is convenient to pack saddlebags, panniers and all the loose bits in a bag together. You are permitted one item of hand baggage approximately 20 × 20 × 45cm and theoretically less than 5kg; sadd-lebags should fit. Keep tools in your hand baggage. Camping stove cartridges and liquid fuel may not be carried at all; matches may only be carried on the person. Make sure that the travel agent makes a note on your booking that you will be taking a bicycle with you and allow an extra half hour at check-in for any dismantling.

Fig. 86 One example of a cycle-carrying roof-rack, by Paddy Hopkirk. Upside-down racks are quick to load and unload (and you'd have to be perverse to forget the front wheel) but need more adjustment of spacing for different-sized bicycles than right-way-up ones

Water

Most internal car and foot ferries within the British Isles will carry bicycles, with wide variations in the ratio of passenger to bicycle fare. On car ferries you usually wheel your bicycle on, put it where the crew indicate, and wheel it off at the other end. On foot ferries you may have to do rather more humping. The *CTC Handbook* gives as far as possible up-to-date information on ferry services and charges—par-ticularly necessary in the far north and west of Scotland, above all if you plan to visit any of the islands. The Caledonian Macbrayne timetable gives fuller details of timings and possible island-hopping trips. Many motorway bridges over estuaries and rivers have free cycle-paths as well; notable examples are the Severn, Tamar, Humber, Medway, Forth, Tay, Clyde and (Bristol) Avon bridges. Clyde, Tyne and some Thames tunnels also take bicycles.

All cross-Channel and North Sea and Irish Sea car ferry services will carry bicycles, at fares varying from free of charge upwards. Once again you wheel the bicycle aboard and off at the other end. Some hover-craft services will carry bicycles.

Road

There are several specially made roof racks available to carry bicycles either right way up, possibly with the front wheel removed, or upside down. If a variety of bicycles is to be carried, right-way-up racks are preferable: nearly all bicycles have a roughly comparable wheelbase whereas the distance between saddle and handlebars varies over a much wider range. It is also possible to carry bicycles upside down on an ordinary luggage rack or on two ladder bars using four toestraps per machine, two to hold handlebars and two to hold the saddle. Make sure that the bicycles are securely held to the rack, the rack to the car and the load limit for the roof observed. Roof-borne bicycles can affect the handling of the car. Allow extra time for the journey. Remove loose items such as pumps, bottles and bags before fixing the bicycle to the rack.

In many estate cars bicycles will lie flat with front wheels removed. It is inelegant, and quite possibly illegal, to carry bicycles in car boots with bits poking out.

Now where?

I have avoided in this book suggesting specific routes; I hope that you have been given enough clues to work out the answers for yourself. The book has naturally been biased towards British practice—and if you live in Britain it's natural that you will want to see something of the variety of your own country first. Britain has a range of countryside which cannot be found anywhere else within such a small compass. As you progress from the south-east, from lowland England, north-westwards, you pass through country of increasing grandeur, culminating in the mountains of the Scottish Highlands. But between there is everything—almost—from the horizontal lines and towering skies of the Fens to the lunar landscapes of the north of Skye, by way of the tight and intimate landscapes of softer rural England and the river valleys and open heights of Wales.

But your travels need not stop at Britain's shores. Every year cycle-tourists set off from ports and airports to cycle in most countries of the world, among the grander snow-capped peaks of the Alps or Rockies, or to challenging deserts or tidy Bavarian landscapes—the choice is almost unlimited. They may be mere filigree wheels on a simple machine, but they can take you a long, long way . . .

Fig. 87 A bicycle can be a passport to almost anywhere.
These riders are on a mountain road 1800 metres up,
approaching the Pré de Madame Carle, deep in the heart of
the Massif des Ecrins in the French Alps

APPENDIX I

USEFUL ORGANISATIONS

Useful organisations

CTC (Cyclists' Touring Club), Cotterell House, 69 Meadrow, Godalming, Surrey GU7 3HS (telephone: 04868 7217/8).

'Britain's national cyclists' association—working for all cyclists' reads the CTC's slogan, summing up the Club's active participation in rights and planning matters. The CTC is the principal cycling body consulted when legislation is contemplated and also represents cycling interests on many campaigning, safety, technical and amenity bodies. For members, further benefits include: *Cycletouring* magazine (see Appendix 2); access to the combined knowledge and advice of the Touring, Technical and Legal Departments (who also produce regularly updated information sheets on a wide range of places and topics); Legal Aid if necessary; automatic cycling third-party insurance; cycle insurance scheme; negotiated privileged access to certain forest and other roads and tracks; automatic entitlement to take part in the activities of any of the CTC's 200-plus locally-organised sections. Membership is on an individual or household basis, with certain reductions for 'unwaged' categories. A subsidiary company, CTC Sales Ltd, operates the CTC Shop—particularly good for books and maps—from the same address.

Youth Hostels Association (England and Wales), Trevelyan House, 8 St Stephen's Hill, St Albans, Herts AL1 2DY (telephone: 0727 55215).

Scottish Youth Hostels Association, 7 Glebe Crescent, Stirling FK8 2JA (telephone: 0786 2821).

Youth Hostels Association of Northern Ireland, 56 Bradbury Place, Belfast BT7 1RU (telephone: 0232 224733).

Between them these organisations run over 350 hostels in the United Kingdom. To use hostels you must be a member of the Association of the country in which you are normally resident or have an International Youth Hostels Federation membership card, which costs a lot more. You can join at most hostels, as well as national and regional offices, plus a number of other centres. Each Association produces an annual *Handbook* showing where its hostels are. UK membership cards are valid abroad.

Workshops, classes and cycling clubs

Even the most definitive of textbooks cannot rival actually being shown how to do such things as repairs and maintenance. There are two main sources of such experienced teaching: relatively formally in evening classes or workshops, and rather less so from other members of a CTC local section or a cycling club. Your local library or council information service should be able to tell you where to find any of these. Most independent clubs are affiliated to the BCF (**British Cycling Federation**—the body which controls road and track racing, 16 Upper Woburn Place, London WC1N 0QE) and those with flourishing non-competitive activities are likely to be affiliated to the CTC as well.

The Rough-Stuff Fellowship; details from John Matthews, 9 Liverpool Avenue, Ainsdale, Southport PR8 3NE.

National Off-Road Bicycle Association (NORBA); details from 3 The Shrubbery, Albert Street, St Georges, Telford, Shropshire.

The two organisations interested in off-road cycling. The RSF publishes bi-monthly the *Rough-Stuff Journal* with a remarkable range of practicable (and impracticable) routes. NORBA is devoted to mountain bikes and covers both competitive and non-competitive off-road cycling.

The Tandem Club; details from Mrs C. Blackman, 8 Newnham Road, Hook, Basingstoke, Hants.

Formed originally to enable difficultly-replaceable spares to be made to order in reasonable numbers, the Club now flourishes and publishes *The Tandem Club Journal* every two months to keep members in touch. It

Fig. 88 The idea of group riding with a CTC section or cycling club may not appeal to everyone, but within such sections or clubs there is a wealth of collective experience of equipment, maintenance and bicycle travel which will be freely on offer to the newcomer

still has its spares service. There are some local and national meets and weekends. Membership is on an individual or, of course, a couple basis.

The Association of Lightweight Campers,
c/o 11 Lower Grosvenor Place, London SW1W 0EY.

The Association now exists as a section of the **Camping and Caravanning Club** and members have to be members of the parent body first; the additional Association fee is nominal. The Association issues a *Bulletin* every two months with site, social and technical information.

Accommodation

There is now a wealth of accommodation listings available, probably the most comprehensive being available from local authority information services and from the various regional tourist boards. The latters' lists include everything from top hotels to campsites. Details of where these are located may be obtained from the English Tourist Board, 4 Grosvenor Gardens, London SW1 (telephone: 01–730 3400); the Wales Tourist Board, Welcome House, High Street, Llandaff, Cardiff (0222 567701); the Isle of Man Tourist Board, 13 Victoria Street, Douglas (0624 4323); the Scottish Tourist Board, 23 Ravelston Terrace, Edinburgh 4 (031–332 2433); and the Northern Ireland Tourist Board, River House, 48 High Street, Belfast BT1 2DS (0232 246609), as appropriate. In addition the CTC handbook is useful for information on accommodation.

APPENDIX II

MAGAZINES AND BOOKS

Magazines

The news: *Cycling Weekly* (published by Business Press International, Prospect House, Cheam, Surrey) The cyclist's Thursday newspaper with a strong racing bias—there is more touring coverage outside the racing season. Extensive ads plus equipment news and features. Good and rapid for private sales/wants.

The glossies: *Bicycle Action* (136–8 New Cavendish Street, London W1. Monthly) and *Bicycle Magazine* (Cover Publications, PO Box 381, Mill Harbour, London E14. Monthly) High-tech and equipment-biased, lively, colourful, competitive. At the time this book was being written they were deep into mountain bikes and triathlons but showing signs of emerging. Regular equipment reviews.

The rather-less-shiny: *Bicycle Times* (Kelthorn Ltd, 26 Commercial Buildings, Dunston, Gateshead. Monthly) *Cycling World* (Stone Industrial Publications, Andrew House, 2a Granville Road, Sidcup, Kent. Monthly) Touring-biased and directed more towards the conventional cycling club world. Equipment features and reviews.

The specialist: *Cycletouring* (CTC, 69 Meadrow, Godalming, Surrey. Every two months) The magazine of the CTC, free to members but also available on subscription to non-members. Official and local CTC news, reports on CTC's rights work, touring features, lots of readers' letters, equipment reviews and news, small ads.

Books

There have been quite a lot of cycling books over the last century or so, particularly ones dealing with the competitive side. The brief personal selection below includes titles which may be of use and interest to readers of this book. The two main mail order outlets for cycling books—the CTC Shop (see Appendix 1) and Selpress Ltd, PO Box 146, Hemel Hempstead, Herts HP3 0RA—have far more extensive lists.

Libraries usually stock cycling and travel books and, if not, can certainly obtain them for you—which may be the only way of reading titles which are out of print. Most libraries mark and arrange books in numerical order according to the Dewey Decimal Classification or a variant of it. Bicycle and related books are classified as follows:
629.2272 Bicycles; 629.231 Bicycle design; 629.28872 Bicycle maintenance and repair. 790.09423 Recreation facilities, including use of national and country parks. 796.01960941 Sport for physically handicapped persons. 796.54 Camping. 796.6 Cycling; 796.609 History of cycling. 912.04 Map reading. 914.1 Great Britain (incorporating 914.104857 Description, travel and guides); 914.11 Scotland; 914.12 to 914.14 Scottish regions; 914.2 England; 914.21 to 914.28 English regions; 914.29 Wales; 914.291 to 914.299 Welsh regions. Ordnance Survey maps (most libraries have at least the 1:50000 Landrover series) are also filed around this point.

GENERAL
City Rider: How to survive with your bike
By Nigel Thomas; published by Elm Tree Books, 1981; ISBN 0 241 10575 7 (pbk) A lively introduction to leisure cycling and far wider-ranging than the title suggests.

Richard's Bicycle Book
By Richard Ballantine; published by Pan Books; ISBN 0 330 26766 3 (pbk) A well-known and enthusiastic introduction to cycling, and especially good on maintenance. Sadly, external pressures have forced the deletion of the stirring pages in earlier editions devoted to deterring dogs from leaning too far on the side of the cyclist.

Bicycling Science
By Frank R. Whitt and David G. Wilson; published by MIT Press, 1982 (2nd ed); ISBN 0 262 23111 5 (hbk), 0 262 73060 X (pbk) A survey of measurements of the properties and performance of bicycles and cyclists, together with some theoretical considerations.

The Penguin Book of the Bicycle
By Roderick Watson and Martin Gray; published by
Penguin Books, 1978; ISBN 0 14 004297 0 (pbk)
A rather disorganised, almost random, mix of cycling
lore, mechanics, history and anecdote—with many
further references. A good source book.

Fat Man on a Bicycle
By Tom Vernon; published by Collins, 1982; ISBN 0
00 636529 9 (pbk)
The edited account based on a BBC radio series of a
journey across France by bicycle.

Wheels of Choice
By Tim Hughes; published by Cyclographic Publications; ISBN 0 907191 01 1 (pbk)
A collection of cycle-touring photographs and sparse
text assembled under a title which is obviously a dead
crib from H. G. Wells.

ROAD CONDUCT
The Highway Code
Published by HMSO; ISBN 0 11 550700 0 (pbk)

Know your Traffic Signs
Published by HMSO; ISBN 0 11 550550 4 (pbk)

FICTION
Cycling
Compiled by Jeanne Mackenzie; published by Oxford
University Press in their Little Oxford Books series,
1981; ISBN 0 19 214117 1 (hbk)
An anthology of cycling items from a century's worth
of literature and journalism.

Three Men on the Bummel
By Jerome K. Jerome; published by Dent in their
Everyman series; ISBN 0 460 00188 4 (hbk), 0 460
01188 X (pbk)
This less well-known sequel to the same three charac-
ters' adventures in a boat was written in 1900 and
describes a rather rambling bicycle tour in the Black
Forest.

The Wheels of Chance
By H. G. Wells; published by Dent in their Everyman
series; ISBN 0 460 01914 7 (pbk)
The turn-of-the-century tale of how Mr Hoopdriver
forsook the draper's counter for the bicycle and the
open road and made the acquaintance of the Girl in
Grey.

The Bicycle in Life, Love, War and Literature
By Seamus McGonagle; published by Pelham Books;
o/p
An anthology of miscellaneous cycling pieces.

MAINTENANCE
Sutherland's Handbook for Bicycle Mechanics
By Howard Sutherland; obtainable in the UK from
Selpress Books (above) or Ron Kitching (see Appendix
3)
The definitive—and correspondingly expensive—
American work.

Two other books with good maintenance sections are
Richard's Bicycle Book (above) and *Bicycle* by John
Wilcockson; published by Marshall Cavendish, 1980;
ISBN 0 88421 156 8 (hbk). The latter has 45 pages on the
topic with plentiful line drawings and advice on such
things as chainsets with cotter-pins.

A useful recent publication, which, although describ-
ing mainly racing bicycles, covers principles common
to all types is *Bicycle Mechanics in Workshop and
Competition* by Steve Snowling and Ken Evans; published by Springfield Books, 1986; ISBN 0 947655
14X.

MAPS AND TRAVEL
Ordnance Survey Maps: A descriptive manual
By J. B. Harley; published by the Ordnance Survey,
1975; ISBN 0 319 00000 1 (hbk)

Cyclist's Britain
Edited by Andrew Duncan and Mel Petersen; pub-
lished by Pan Books and the Ordnance Survey, 1985;
ISBN 0 330 28610 2 (pbk)
A selection of cycling routes in England, Wales and
Scotland suggested by active cyclists and keyed to the
OS 1:250 000 map.

Cycling in Europe
By Nick Crane; published by Oxford Illustrated Press,
1984; ISBN 0 330 28547 (pbk), 0 902 28077 5 (hbk)
First-hand information on cycle-touring in the countries of Europe.

CAMPING
Modern Lightweight Camping
By Pat and Hazel Constance; published by Robert
Hale, 1985; ISBN 0 7090 1751 0 (hbk), 0 7090 1868 1
(pbk)
A comprehensive guide to lightweight camping equip-
ment and how to get the best out of it.

Three books which are not cycling books but which give some interesting ideas for travel away from metalled roads are:

The Drovers' Roads of Wales
By Fay Godwin and Shirley Toulson; published by Wildwood House, 1977; ISBN 0 7045 0251 8 (hbk)
An exploration of some of the old green roads of mid and North Wales.

The Oldest Road
By J. R. L. Anderson and Fay Godwin; published by Wildwood House, 1975; ISBN 0 7045 0167 8 (hbk), 0 7045 0168 6 (pbk)
A detailed guide to the Ridgeway which runs the length of the Berkshire Downs.

Walking the Scottish Highlands: General Wade's Military Roads
By Tom Ang and Michael Pollard; published by André Deutsch, 1985; ISBN 0 233 97620 5 (hbk)
The title says 'walking' but much of this one-time thousand-mile network is eminently cyclable.

BRANDS AND SUPPLIERS OF EQUIPMENT

Brands and suppliers of equipment

This list bring together items of equipment and some suppliers of services, most of which are mentioned by name in the text. Some suppliers deal with a wider range than shown here but only the items listed have been cited in specific contexts. In most cases equipment is available only through the normal retail trade and no address is therefore given. Addresses *are* given where you may deal with the supplier direct or, in the cases marked 'I', where the supplier will provide information or brochures on items which they make or import and then distribute through retail outlets.

AFA-*Christophe* (toeclips)

Atom (hubs—brand name of Maillard)

Aztec (brake cables, brake blocks)

Bartholomew, John (maps, atlases), The Edinburgh Geographical Institute, Duncan Street, Edinburgh (I)

Been Bag (clothing), No. 1, Industrial Estate, Medomsley Road, Consett, Co Durham (I)

Bike Ribbon (handlebar tape)

Jim Blackburn (pannier carriers)

David Bolton (sidecars, trailers), Lloyds Bank Gardens, Market Square, Princes Risborough, Bucks

Bridgeport Brass Ltd ('Cure-c-Cure' feather-edge tyre patches)

Brooks (leather saddles—brand-name of Sturmey-Archer)

Bulldog (camping cooking pans)

Byka (tyre-tread driven dynamos and lighting systems)

Campagnolo (hubs, head bearings, chainsets, pedals, seat pillars, gears, tools—and a fancy crokscrew!)

Camping Gaz (camping stoves, butane cartridges)

Carradice (bags), St Mary's Street, Nelson, Lancs BB9 7BA (I)

Castrol (lubricants)

Cinelli (handlebar bends and stems, saddles (Unica brand name))

CJ Designs (handlebar map carrier), obtainable through CTC Shop (Appendix 1)

Claud Butler (complete touring bicycles)

Coleman (petrol camping stoves, fuel)

Cyclo Gear Co (cable clips, bolt-on saddlebag strap eyes for bag-loopless saddles, fixed sprockets, tools)

Dawes (complete touring bicycles)

DEB Chemical Proprietaries (Swarfega hand-cleaning jelly)

Dia-Compe (brakes, levers, special two-cable lever)

Esge (mudguards)

Emmepi (bottle cages)

Evans, F. W. (complete touring bicycles), 77/79 The Cut, Waterloo, London SE1

Ever-Ready (batteries, battery lamps, bulbs)

George Fitt Engineering (tricycles for the partially disabled), Westmead Road, Whitstable, Kent

Gore-Tex ('breathable' waterproof fabric—brand name of W. L. Gore)

Bill Hannington ('Rann'-type trailer on which child pedals behind bicycle or tandem), 34 Marshland Square, Emmer Green, Reading, Berks

Happy Eater (franchise chain of roadside café/ restaurants; branches have free map showing situation of others in the chain)

Helly Hansen (polypropylene thermal underwear— brand name Lifa)

Bob Jackson (tricycles, tandems), 148 Harehills Lane, Leeds

Karrimor (bags, carriers, Karrimat closed-cell foam camping insulating mats), Avenue Parade, Accrington, Lancs (I)

Kitchen Devil (serrated edge knife)

Kitching, Ron (importer of *inter alia* TA, Mavic, Milremo and Sun Tour products; produces detailed catalogue *Everything Cycling* which is useful reference), Hookstone Park, Harrogate, Yorkshire (I)

Laprade (seat pillars)

Little Chef (franchise chain of roadside café/ restaurants; branches have free map showing situation of others in the chain)

George Longstaff (tandems, tricycles, specialised parts and conversions for disabled riders), 80 Newchapel Road, Rookery, Kidsgrove, Stoke-on-Trent

Lyotard (pedals)

Mafac (brakes, including brazed-on cantilever models)

Maillard (hubs, freewheels)

Map Trap (map holder produced by CJ Designs)

Mavic (rims, hubs)

Mercian (tandems, complete touring bicycles), 28 Stenson Road, Cavendish, Derby

Michelin (tyres, tubes—and, in France, maps)

Milremo (accessories)

Moulton, Alex (lightweight small-wheel bicycles), Bradford-on-Avon, Wiltshire (I)

Nachman, Arthur (shoes—under Arturo brand-name)

Nisi (rims)

Normandy (hubs—brand-name of Maillard)

Opticycle Fibre (optical fibre allowing check on illumination of rear light), Capricorn Contracts Ltd, 18 Beeston Road, Kinnerston, Chester

Optimus (paraffin pressure and petrol camping stoves)

Ordnance Survey (maps), Romsey Road, Maybush, Southampton (I)

Pashley (tricycles including child-carrying models), Masons Road, Stratford-on-Avon, Warwickshire

Pennine Outdoor (do-it-yourself fabrics for bags, clothing and camping items), Hardknott, Holmbridge, Huddersfield

Peugeot (complete touring bicycles)

Phoenix Mountaineering (tents, sleeping bags), Coquetdale Trading Estate, Amble, Morpeth, Northumberland (I)

Pointfive (sleeping bags)

Regina (freewheels, chains)

Rema Tip-Top (feather-edge tyre patches)

Renold (chains)

Reynolds Cycles (shoes), 159–161 Wellingborough Road, Northampton

Reynolds (531 and 501 cycle frame tubing), TI Reynolds 531 Ltd, PO Box 765, Hay Hall, Redfern Road, Tyseley, Birmingham (I)

Rice, Ronald (Pedalaid swinging crank adaptation for disabled riders), 18c de Parys Avenue, Bedford

Rogers, Ken (tricycles, including adaptations for disabled riders), 71 Berkeley Avenue, Cranford, Hounslow, Middx

Sakae Ringyo (SR) (handlebar bends and stems, pedals, cranks and chainwheels, seat pillars)

Salisbury, Pete (shoes), 30a Avenue Road, Rushden, Northants

Sanyo (tyre-tread driven dynamos)

Saunders, Robert (tents), Five Oaks Lane, Chigwell, Essex (I)

Sedisport (chains)

Shimano (hubs, gears, pedals)

Silca ('track'-type pump with gauge)

SKS (frame-fitting pumps)

Spencer (mudguards)

SR = Sakae Ringyo

Strong (seat pillars)

Stronglight (cranks and chainwheels)

Sturmey Archer (Brooks saddles)

Sugino (chainwheels and cranks)

Sun Tour (gear mechanisms, freewheels, hubs)

Super Champion (rims—brand-name of Wolber)

Swallow (tricycles, junior pedalling attachments, crank shorteners), 2 Stannets, Laindon North Trade Centre, Essex

Swarfega (hand-cleaning jelly—the brand-name of DEB)

TA (cranks and chainwheels, pedals, front bags, front bag carrier)

Tilley (gas camping stoves, resealable butane cartridges)

Tonard (front and rear bag carriers)

Tor (do-it-yourself fabrics for bags, clothing and camping items), 3 Fryer Street, The Market, Runcorn, Cheshire

Trangia (methylated spirit camping stoves)

Ultimate Equipment (tents, sleeping bags), Ryburne Mill, Hanson Lane, Halifax, West Yorkshire (I)

Unica (plastic saddles—brand-name of Cinelli)

Vango (tents), 70 East Hamilton Street, Ladyburn, Greenock (I)

Weinmann (brakes, rims)

Whisker, J. D. (comprehensive accessory mail order service—list available), 684A Goffs Lane, Goffs Oak, Waltham Cross, Herts EN7 5BR

Wolber (tyres, Super Champion rims)

Wonder (batteries, lights)

Zefal ('track'-type pump with gauge)

Zeus (hubs, tools)

APPENDIX IV

TOURING CHECKLISTS

Checklists

These lists are intended as reminders, to check that
you haven't forgotten anything—which is why they
look rather formidable. You will have to form your
own judgement on what you actually need on any
particular occasion, bearing in mind season, weather,
terrain, distance and so on. I have marked with a ●
items I would consider essential. Note that the three
lists are *cumulative*: that is to say, consult the first and
second lists for a tour, and all three for a camping tour.

Out for the day

On the bicycle
● Pump
   Drinking bottle/vacuum flask
   Front and rear lights (check working order)

Tools and spares
● Spare *airtight* inner tube of the right size (or two)
● Tyre levers (three)
● Puncture repair outfit (containing patches, rubber
   solution, abrasive paper, tyre patching canvas)
● Wheel spanner (5/16 × 3/8 BSF—not needed if
   quick-release hubs are fitted)
● 4–5–6mm allen keys
● 8–9, 10–11mm spanners
● Rear brake inner wire (can be used as spare for
   front too, with excess coiled up)
   Swarfega (in small tin)
   Spare lamp bulbs (padded in small canister such as
   35mm film can)
   Spare batteries

Clothing
● Extra pullover or tracksuit top
   Headgear/waterproof headgear
● Handkerchief
   Gloves/track mitts
● Cape or cagoule

Other
● Lock and key
● Map(s)
● Money/cheque book/credit or charge cards/coins
   for telephone calls
   Sunglasses
   Any addresses or phone numbers you need (such
   as where you're going to meet your friends)
● Personal identity and contact addresses/phone
   numbers
   Saddle cover (to protect from wet when parked
   outside)
● Emergency high-calorie food
● First-aid kit, comprising at least
   sealed sterile dressings (e.g. Melalin)
   adhesive tape (e.g. Micropore)
   antiseptic (e.g. TCP)
   cotton wool
   triangular bandage and 4 or 5 5cm safety pins
   clean needle
   cutting instrument (scalpel blade, razor blade)
   small scissors

Away for the night—or longer

Tools and spares
Crank fitting and extractor tools (to fit model used)
Small screwdriver/cross-head screwdriver
Chain bearing pin (rivet) extractor
Punch/drift
Freewheel remover (to fit model used)
Spoke nipple key
Rear gear cable inner wire (can be used as spare for
front too, with excess coiled up)
Spare spokes of right length for both wheels
Spare brake blocks or blocks in shoes
Odd nuts and bolts (especially mudguard,
chainwheel)
Plastic insulating tape
Pair of toestraps/elastic straps
Small oilcan/pot of grease

Length of 18–20swG copper or soft iron wire (for emergency mudguard or similar repairs)

Clothing
Underwear/thermal vests
Shirts/T-shirts/cycling tops
Shorts
Socks (ankle or long, as appropriate)
'Plusses'/tracksuit bottoms
Change of trousers/jeans/skirt for evenings
Slippers/sandals/soft shoes
Long johns/thermal legs/acrylic tights
Sleeping wear
Sheet sleeping bag (if hostelling)
Handkerchiefs

Toilet kit
Soap
Towel (two small towels are better than one larger one, especially for camping)
Razor/nailbrush/comb/hairbrush/shampoo
Toothbrush/toothpaste
Insect repellant/uv-screening cream

Eating
Knife/fork/dessert spoon/teaspoon/Kitchen Devil
Tea towel
Can opener/crown cork remover/corkscrew
Food

Other
Needle/thread/safety pins
Polyethylene bags/stuff sacs
Membership cards (yha/syha, ctc etc)
Accommodation lists/yha/syha handbook
Travel tickets/passport/insurance documents/currency/travellers' cheques

Camping

Sleeping
Tent (with poles, pole A-pieces, pegs, any necessary guylines)
Karrimat
Sleeping bag
Small torch (unless you have bicycle battery lamps)

Cooking and eating
Stove/gas cartridge/spare fuel (*not* the latter two if travelling by air)
Matches/lighter (must be carried on person if travelling by air; matches best in waterproof container)
Extra tent pegs for securing stove
Pans/lifting handle/short wooden spatula for cooking
Mug/plate
Pot scourer/cleaning sponge/washing-up liquid
Extra drinking bottle/collapsible bucket or water container
Water purifying tablets

Other
Extra elastic straps
10-metre length of guyline for clothes drying/clothes pegs
Toilet paper (flat pack easier to carry than roll)
Some sort of footwear for padding round damp fields (thick-soled sandals are as good as anything)
Sheet of heavy-gauge polyethylene about 1.5 × 1 metre (has all sorts of uses for keeping things off damp ground or covering bikes overnight)
Even more polyethylene bags

INDEX

Entries marked (US) are the American terms for which British equivalents are given

Index